TOASTS

ONE-WORD DEFINITIVE BOOKS BY PAUL DICKSON

Chow

Drunk

Jokes

Names

Slang

Timelines

Toasts

Words

Paul Dickson

Toasts

OVER 1,500 OF THE BEST TOASTS,

SENTIMENTS, BLESSINGS, AND GRACES

BLOOMSBURY

NEW YORK · LONDON · NEW DELHI · SYDNEY

Published by Bloomsbury USA, New York

All papers used by Bloomsbury USA are natural, recyclable products
made from wood grown in well-managed forests. The manufacturing
processes conform to the environmental regulations of the country of origin.

LIBRARY OF CONGRESS CATALOGING-IN-PUBLICATION DATA
HAS BEEN APPLIED FOR

ISBN 978-1-60819-065-2

Image credits: Pages 59 and 60, the Museum of Modern Art/Film
Stills Archive. Page 86, Library of Congress, Prints and
Photographs Division. Page 196, NASA.

Originally published in different form in 1981 by Delacorte Press,
then in a revised edition in 1991 by Crown Publishers, Inc.
This newly revised edition published in 2009.

5   7   9   10   8   6   4

Designed by Sara E. Stemen
Typeset by Westchester Book Group
Printed and bound in the U.S.A. by Thomson-Shore Inc., Dexter, Michigan

HERE'S
TO THE
TOAST

. . . and to the reader, in the form of a toast from Edith Lea Chase and W. E. P. French's genre classic of 1905, *Waes Hael*:

A health, O reader, and 'tis our adieu:
Good luck, good health, good fortune wait on you.
Over the wine please note our loving look:—
Waes Hael! Hoch! Skoal! Prosit! Buy the book.

Contents

Introduction

"Next to the originator of a good sentence is the first quoter of it."
—RALPH WALDO EMERSON

THERE ARE A number of old things that we are well rid of—child labor, the Berlin wall, scurvy, glass shampoo bottles, and too many others to mention—but there are still others that we are foolish to let slip away. Toasting is one of the latter.

A toast is a basic form of human expression that can be used to convey virtually any emotion, from love to rage (although raging toasts tend to cross the line into the realm of curses). They can be sentimental, cynical, lyrical, comical, defiant, long, short—even just a single word.

The names and traditions associated with the custom are many and date back to the ancient world. Toasts are also very much a part of our literary heritage and, with the exception of the past few decades, there has not been a writer of note from Milton to Mencken who has not left us at least one good toast. What's more, some of our favorite fictional characters have uttered classics—among them, Tiny Tim's "God bless us every one!" from Dickens's *A Christmas Carol* and Rick's "Here's lookin' at you, kid!" from the 1942 movie *Casablanca*.

Most important, however, is that toasts are so useful. They are a medium through which deep feelings of love, hope, high spirits, and admiration can be quickly, conveniently, and sincerely expressed.

There was a time, not that long ago, when one could not go to a luncheon—let alone a banquet or wedding—without hearing a series of carefully proposed and executed toasts. Toasts were the mark of one's ability to come up with appropriate, inspiring words in honor of some person, sentiment, or institution. It really didn't matter whether the toast was an original written for the occasion or a time-tested classic passed down from the Elizabethan era. What did matter was whether the toast kept the proceedings moving at a jolly pace.

About halfway into the twentieth century, however, the custom of creative, thoughtful toasting began to erode. It seemed that people had less time and inclination to compose or memorize them. And this decline wasn't limited to the United States. British author John Pudney wrote in 1963 of the "decline in the eloquence and variety of the toast in the English language. The last two generations at least seem to find themselves embarrassed by the formality of toasting."

In recent decades, the decline has continued to the point at which a set of wedding toasts may have no more style, grace, or imagination than a clearing of the throat and a hastily yelped "Here's to the bride and groom! Here's to Fred and Maxine!" Moreover, most of the workaday toasts still in use are of the quick, down-the-hatch variety that reduces the custom to a mumbled word (Cheers! Prosit!) or phrase (Happy days! Hair on your chest!) uttered more from habit than any real sentiment. The World Wide Web, which should have been a boon to toasting, turned into a mixed blessing—suddenly more material was available, but much of it was crude or obscene, suited to fraternity house drunkathons and biker bars, not important occasions.

At the same time, some of the better old toasts have become virtually meaningless, either because they have been shortened or they have lost their original context. The ubiquitous "Here's mud in your eye!" is a good case in point. A fuller, much older version ends with "while I look over your lovely sweetheart!" In the days when the American West was opening up, "Mud in your eye" had an entirely different context: A pioneering farmer about to leave the East would stop in the local tavern to say good-bye to friends, who would propose the toast in hopes the farmer would find soft, rich, and damp soil that would be thrown up as specks of mud as he plowed it.

Toasting is still an important custom on such formal occasions as state dinners and diplomatic receptions. Yet, in this realm, a different kind of erosion has taken place. Official toasts—which have always tended to be light, friendly, and anecdotal—have become vehicles for long, windy political addresses.

Things really began to sour in 1975, when Zambian president

Kenneth Kaunda startled guests at a White House dinner by responding to a traditional toast from President Gerald Ford with a twenty-minute "toast" stating his nation's foreign policy. (Ford was not beyond the occasional gaffe, as in this toast to Anwar Sadat in December 1975: "[To] the great people and the government of Israel—Egypt, excuse me." And in December 1982, President Ronald Reagan rose at a dinner hosted in his honor by the president of Brazil and proposed a toast to "the people of Bolivia.")

In 1978, a toasting low point of sorts was achieved when Marshal Tito of Yugoslavia bested Kuanda with a rambling forty-minute dissertation on his views of the international political scene. Shortly thereafter, the forty-five-minute barrier fell, and it seemed the hourlong toast would become a reality. In the early 1980s, the U.S. State Department's Office of Protocol began to suggest routinely that all White House toasts last no more than three minutes, but the suggestions were soon ignored. The morning after a June 1986 toast at the White House by Uruguayan president Julio María Sanguinetti, the *Washington Post* diplomatically said: "Sanguinetti's toast was notable for its length and historical detail."

Not only is conviviality missing from such "toasts," but some are downright hostile. In early 1979, when President Jimmy Carter and President José López Portillo of Mexico traded a well-publicized set of diplomatic insults in Mexico City, they called their attacks "toasts." Portillo ungraciously began the exchange with a wide-ranging indictment of the United States, and a dazed Carter jabbed back with a tasteless recollection of a bout of Montezuma's revenge. Later in his administration Carter actually included a question-and-answer session as part of a toast.

Enough. The point is that we have come close to abandoning a useful medium and form of communication in an age of media and communication. Simply stated, the purpose of this book is, among other things, to help as a vehicle for a revival.

In truth, some bright omens and recent developments signal a renewed interest in toasting. When the first version of this book was published in 1981, Ronald Reagan was the new president, the Berlin wall was in place, MTV and the IBM PC made their debuts, and women had just gained the right to enter McSorley's, the tavern in Manhattan's East Village where, for more than a century, female visitors had been greeted with the clanging of a fight bell and swift, unceremonious expulsion. There was no e-mail (at least not for people outside the U.S. military) and the World Wide Web was still a vague abstraction. Starbucks, Nike, Wal-Mart, and Target did not exist, nor were there cell phones, minivans, SUVs, laptops, or a hundred other things that now define our world.

The most notable development has been the use of the toast as a signal for warming relationships between nations, rather than as an excuse for a diatribe. In early 1984, a seven-hundred-word toast to Chinese-American friendship by Premier Zhao Ziyang became the basis for a nuclear-cooperation treaty between the two nations; critics of the resulting treaty accused President Reagan of conducting "diplomacy by dinner toast." Later in the decade, the progress in U.S.-Soviet relations was marked with jovial toasting between leaders, and in the fall of 1990 the visible proof of the official reunification of Germany was a photo of the leaders of the two Germanys posed with raised glasses.

When this book's second edition was published in 1991, people were beginning to think about toasting in the new millennium. One that unfortunately missed the mark was "The coming millennium: When great men are honest and honest men are great."

In the early part of the twenty-first century, toasts have become increasingly terse and purposeful—especially those delivered in public for the television cameras. "Let me propose a toast," said President Barack Obama at a state dinner on February 22, 2009, in a prime example of the short-but-sweet school of toasting, "to the nation's governors, to the United States of America, and to the certain hope that despite our current travails, that we will all emerge more prosperous and more unified than we were before."

So, here's to it! And to fuel and give this revival an extra boost, the following pages contain more than fifteen hundred of the best, most useful, and most literate toasts that could be found. With the help of dozens of people—reference librarians, museum curators, brewers, distillers, vintners, and old friends—I have been able to collect something on the order of six thousand toasts, from which the examples in this book were culled.

A Brief History of Raised Glasses

THE CUSTOM OF drinking a "health" to the prosperity, happiness, luck, or good health of another dates back into antiquity—and, perhaps, into prehistory.

It is impossible to point to the moment when the first crude vessel was raised in honor of an ancient god or to the health of a newborn baby. Nor do we have any idea when a parched traveler first lifted a cup in thanks to the man or woman who gave him wine.

What we do know is that the custom of drinking to another's health permeated the ancient world. Odysseus drank to the health of Achilles in the *Odyssey*. An early Greek custom called for a pledge of three cups—one to Hermes, one to the Graces, and one to Zeus. In Rome, drinking to another's health became so important the Senate decreed that diners must drink to Augustus at every meal. Fabius Maximus declared that the Romans should not eat or drink before praying for him and drinking to his health.

The ancient Hebrews, Persians, and Egyptians were toasters, as were the Saxons, Huns, and other tribes. In *The Decline and Fall of the Roman Empire*, Edward Gibbon tells of a multicourse feast among the Huns at which their leader Attila led no less than three rounds of toasts for each course.

Over time the simple act of toasting became embellished and intertwined with other customs. (It wasn't until the seventeenth century that the act was actually referred to as a toast. More on that shortly.) At some point along the way, for instance, the gesture of clinking glasses or cups became popular. It has long been believed that this began during the Christian era, as the original intention of the clink was to produce a bell-like noise so as to banish the devil, who was thought to be re-pelled by bells. Another explanation for the glass-clinking custom is the belief that all five senses should come into play to get the greatest pleasure from a drink. It should be tasted, touched, seen, smelled, and—with the clink—heard.

The British added an odd but essential custom to their tippling during the Danish invasion of the tenth century. This was the practice of pledging another's health in the most literal terms—that is, a friend stating the intention of protecting a drinker who is tossing back a drink. This stemmed from the Danes' objectionable habit of cutting the throats of Englishmen as they drank. Shakespeare's line from *Timon of Athens*, "Great men should drink with harness on their throats," is one of several old literary references to this murderous behavior.

Another morbidly fascinating custom from northern Europe is that of drinking mead or ale from the skull of a fallen enemy. The Scots and Scandinavians both practiced this primitive form of recycling, and the Highland Scotch *skiel* (tub) and the Norse *skoal* (bowl) derive from it. The modern toast *skoal* in turn comes from the Old Norse term. This custom persisted through the eleventh century, after which only an occasional skull was converted into a drinking vessel. Lord Byron ac-quired a human skull, had it mounted as drinking vessel, and wrote an inscription for it that read

> Start not—nor deem my spirit fled:
> In me behold the only skull
> From which, unlike a living head,
> Whatever flows is never dull.
>
> I lived, I loved, I quaff'd like thee:
> I died: let earth my bones resign:
> Fill up—thou canst not injure me,
> The worm hath fouler lips than thine.
>
> Better to hold the sparkling grape,
> Than nurse the earthworm's slimy brood;
> And circle in the goblet's shape
> The drink of gods, than reptile's food.

Where once my wit, perchance, hath shone,
In aid of others let me shine;
And when, alas! our brains are gone,
What nobler substitute than wine?

Quaff while thou canst, another race
When thou and thine, like me, are sped,
May rescue thee from earth's embrace,
And rhyme and revel with the dead.

The first *recorded* instance of a toast being offered in England occurred in the year 450 at a great feast given by King Vortigern of Britain to his Saxon allies. Rowena, the beautiful daughter of the Saxon leader Hengist, held up a large goblet filled with a spiced beverage and drank to the king, saying, *"Louerd King, waes hael!"*—"Lord King, be of health!"—to which Vortigern replied, *"Drink, hael."*

According to the account of medieval historian Geoffrey of Monmouth, the festivity did not stop there. In short order, Vortigern kissed Rowena, made passionate love to her, and then bargained with Hengist for her hand. A deal was struck by which Hengist received the province of Kent in exchange for Rowena. Vortigern and Rowena were married that evening.

For at least a thousand years, drinking in Britain was commonly accompanied by the same verbal exchange, although *waes hael* became *wassail*. One of the earliest known Christmas carols, dating from the days of the Norman minstrels, ends with these lines:

Each must drain his cup of wine,
And I the first will toss off mine:
Thus I advise,
Here then I bid you all *Wassail*,
Cursed be he who will not say *Drink hail*.

Over the years the term *wassail* became associated with Christmas and the New Year, times of the greatest festivity, and by the seventeenth century it developed the specific meaning of drinking from a large bowl or loving cup on Christmas Day and Twelfth Night, as well as the drink itself. While people of means prepared their own beverage, groups of poor people commonly went from door to door with an empty bowl, which they expected to be filled at every stop. Some prefaced their request with a medley of Christmas carols, while others chanted something more threatening:

> Come, butler, come fill us a bowl of the best;
> Then we hope that your soul in heaven may rest;
> But if you draw us a bowl of the small,
> Then down shall go butler, bowl and all.

A variation on this custom was for a group to go door to door with a beverage of their own making, for which they would expect to be dearly paid. There were songs for this as well:

> Good dame, here at your door
> Our wassail we begin,
> We are all maidens poor,
> We now pray let us in,
> With our wassail.

Some of the old wassailing songs were little more than toasts set to music:

> Here's to _____ and his right ear,
> God send our maister a Happy New Year;
> A Happy New Year as e'er he did see—
> With my wassailing bowl I drink to thee.

> Here's to _____ and her right eye,
> God send our mistress a good Christmas pie:
> A good Christmas pie as e'er I did see—
> With my wassailing bowl I drink to thee.

The present custom of caroling from door to door derives from this wassailing tradition.

Although people had been drinking to one another for centuries, it wasn't called "toasting" until the seventeenth century, when it was customary to place a piece of toast or a crouton in a drink. This is alluded to in many drinking songs and ditties of the period, including this one published in 1684:

> A toast is like a sot; or what is most
> Comparative, a sot is like a toast;
> For when their substance in liquor sink,
> Both properly are said to be in drink.

According to the *Oxford English Dictionary*, the earliest citation for the word *toast* in English appears in a cookbook circa 1430: "and serve forth all that as tostes"—bread roasted over a fire to a golden-brown crispness. This use of the term derives from the Old French *toster*, "to roast," which stems from Late Latin *tostare*, "to grill, to roast, to barbecue." *Tostare* stems from the Latin verb *torrere*, "to burn as the sun does, to dry out by means of heat."

How, then, did a piece of toast come to mean wishing a person good health by means of a communal drink *and* the person toasted? And how did toast end up in a drink? The exact reasons have been blurred by time, but various hints point to the conclusion that either the bread was believed to improve the flavor of the drink in the manner of a spice or that it was a built-in snack, a bit of token nourishment. Whatever the reason, the practice was common, and soon virtually anything found floating in a drink was referred to as "toast." *Merriam-Webster's Third International Dictionary* says the word is derived "from the use of toasted spiced bread to flavor the wine [during a toast], and the notion that the person honored also added flavor."

The transformation from roasted bread to ceremony occurred during the days of Charles II (1660–1685) in the resort city of Bath, where many went for the ardent spirits and warm mineral waters. The exact moment of the name change was recorded in 1709 in the *Tatler* by Isaac Bickerstaffe:

> It happened that on a publick day a celebrated beauty of those times was in the Cross Bath, and one of the crowd of her admirers took a glass of the water in which the fair one stood and

drank her health to the company. There was in the place a gay fellow, half fuddled, who offered to jump in, and swore though he liked not the liquor, he would have the toast. He was opposed in his resolution; yet this whim gave foundation to the present honour which is done to the lady we mention in our liquor, who has ever since been called a toast.

Toasting was immensely popular during the seventeenth century, especially in the British Isles. "To drink at table," wrote one Englishman, "without drinking to the health of some one special, would be considered drinking on the sly, and as an act of incivility."

This popularity bred excess. The English discovered the Scandinavian custom of drinking not just to everyone present but to all of one's *absent* friends as well. Suddenly, one did not have to limit oneself to the mere twenty drinks normally pledged at a party of twenty.

Each nation developed its own customs—most involving excessive drinking. In Scotland, for instance, it was typical to drink sparingly during the meal, wait for the women to withdraw to the drawing room, and then bring in a large punch bowl filled with whiskey, hot water, and sugar. Goblets or mugs were filled, and each round required a toast, a quick drink, and a turned-over vessel to prove that no liquid remained in it. One scholar of the period wrote, "During the seventeenth and the earlier portion of the eighteenth century, after-dinner drinking was protracted for eight to ten hours."

On important occasions, the toaster mounted his chair, placed his right foot on the table, and bellowed out a favorite sentiment—"May ne'er waur be amang us," "May the pleasures of the evening bear the reflection of the morning," et cetera. This was accompanied by lusty cheering.

The toasting and hoisting that accompanied Scottish weddings were enough to put a cramp in the arm. According to a 1692 account, the process began when the parents of the bride and groom met to make the wedding arrangements. The two families would gather at a point equidistant from their homes and would bring a bottle of whiskey with which, if all went well, the coming wedding would be toasted. Closer to the actual event was the predecessor of today's bachelor party.

The male friends of the bride and the male friends of the groom would meet halfway between the bride's and the groom's houses. Each group would appoint a "champion," and the two men would race, either on horseback or foot, to the bride's house, where the winner would receive a beribboned bottle. The bottle would be brought back to the gathering place to be passed among the assembled men as they drank to the bride's health. Then came the wedding and more toasting and drinking.

This period also produced some strange toasting customs. One practice called for men to show their affection for a woman by stabbing themselves in the arm, mixing their blood in their wine, and drinking to the lady in question. In Shakespeare's *The Merchant of Venice*, the Prince of Morocco alludes to this when he talks of making "an incision for your love," and a song of the time rightly proclaimed,

> I stabbed my arm to drink her health,
> The more fool I, the more fool I.

No less repulsive was the custom, prevalent among university students of the period, of proving one's love by toasting in imaginative but progressively nauseating concoctions. In his *History of Toasting*, the Reverend Richard Valpy French told of how two Oxford students proved their devotion to a beauty named Molly: "One, determined to prove that his love did not stick at trifles, took a spoonful of soot, mixed it with his wine, and drank off the mixture. His companion, determined not to be outdone, brought from his closet a phial of ink, which he drank, exclaiming, 'To triumph and Miss Molly.'"

As if this were not enough, student innovators of the time also hit upon the wretched business of grabbing a woman's shoe, using it to ladle wine from a common bowl, and toasting the shoe's owner. Neither the shoe nor the wine benefited.

Though this was not an age of great subtlety, there was an occasional hint of it. The outlawed Jacobites would publicly, though secretly, drink to their exiled Stuart monarch, Bonnie Prince Charlie, by passing their glass over a bowl of water. Thus, while ostensibly toasting the Hanoverian king George II, they were actually drinking to "the king across the water." Less subtle was this Jacobite toast:

> God bless the King, I mean the Faith's Defender,
> God bless—no harm in blessing—the Pretender,
> But which is Pretender, and which is King?
> God bless us all! that's quite another thing.

If anything, it appears toasting became even more pervasive during the boozy eighteenth and early nineteenth centuries. New institutions emerged, most notably the position of toastmaster. Henry Fielding's *Tom Jones*, published in 1749, references a toastmaster whose duties were to propose and announce toasts. In those days the duties of the toastmaster tended to be refereelike, in that his main function was to give all toasters a fair chance to make a verbal contribution. Then, as now, the prime rule of toastmastering was to keep sober and offend no one.

For the most part, the toasts of this period tended to be short, crisp, and to the point—or as one student of toasting has put it, "These were not an excuse for speeches but for wit and wine." A case in point were the toasts given in the officers' wardroom during the days when Horatio Nelson commanded the Royal Navy. The first toast would always be to the king, with the second (changing each day) prescribed as follows:

> **Monday:** "Our ships at sea."
> **Tuesday:** "Our men."
> **Wednesday:** "Ourselves."
> **Thursday:** "A bloody war or a sickly season."
> **Friday:** "A willing foe and sea room."
> **Saturday:** "Sweethearts and wives."
> **Sunday:** "Absent friends."

In contrast, the toasts of the era's sailors were more poetic:

> The wind that blows, the ship that goes
> And the lass that loves a sailor.

And

Damn his eyes,
If he ever tries
To rob a poor man of his ale.

If the toasts were frugal, the drinking that went with them was anything but. In *Dyott's Diary, 1781–1845*, William Dyott gives an account of a dinner at which the prince regent, afterward George IV, was one of the celebrants.

The prince took the chair himself and ordered me to his Vice. We had a very good dinner and he sent wine of his own, the very best Claret I ever tasted. We had the Grenadiers drawn up in front of the mess-room windows to fire a volley in honour of the troops. As soon as dinner was over he began. He did not drink himself: he always drinks Madiera. He took very good care to see everybody fill, and he gave 23 bumpers [a glass filled to the top] without a halt. In the course of my experience, I never saw such fair drinking. When he had finished his list of bumpers, I begged leave as Vice to give the Superior, and recommended it to the Society to stand up on our chairs with three times three, taking their time from the Vice. I think it was the most laughable sight I ever beheld to see our Governor, our General, and the Commodore all so drunk they could scarce stand on the floor, hoisted up on their chairs with each a bumper in his hand; and the three times three cheers was what they were afraid to attempt for fear of falling. I then proposed his Royal Highness and a good wind whenever he sailed . . . with the same ceremony. He stood at the head of the table during these toasts, and I never saw a man laugh so much in my life. When we had drunk the last, the old Governor desired to know if we had any more as he said if once he got down he should never get up again. His Royal Highness saw we were all pretty well done, and he walked off. There were twenty dined, we drank sixty-three bottles of wine.

Ample evidence suggests that such excess was also common in America. An account from 1770 describes a dinner held in New York for a Captain McDougal and forty-four of his friends. They ate forty-five pounds of steak and drank forty-five toasts. A description of a 1787 New York dinner tells of the diners toasting their way through fifteen kinds of wine and two beers.

In fact, no country seemed to have a lock on such behavior. A popular custom in Edinburgh in the nineteenth century was known as "saving the ladies." Lord Cockburn described it in his journal:

> When after any fashionable assembly the male guests had conducted their fair partners to their homes, they returned to the supper-room. Then one of the number would drink to the health of the lady he professed to admire, and in so doing empty his glass. Another gentleman would name another lady, also drinking a bumper in her honour. The former would reply by swallowing a social glass to his lady, followed by the other, each combatant persisting till one of the two fell upon the floor. Other couples followed in like fashion. These drinking competitions were regarded with interest by gentlewomen who next morning enquired as to the prowess of their champions.

Cockburn, by the way, was horrified by the inane and sentimental lines his contemporaries would utter as "an excuse for the glass." Some of the toasts that most disgusted him were "May the hand of charity wipe away the tears from the eyes of sorrow," "May the pleasure of the evening bear the reflections of the morning," and, saving the worst for last, "The reflection of the moon in the cawn bosom of the lake."

Over the years such excess prompted more than a few decrees, rulings, and antitoast crusades. This opposition merits a moment's digression.

Charles the Great, Maximilian, and Charles V, among others, enacted laws against the custom. Even Louis XIV, not one to be put off by a touch of debauchery, finally forbade the offering of toasts at his court. It is noteworthy that one of the main objectives of the first known temperance society (founded in 1517) was to abolish toasting. In the American Colonies, a law was put into effect in Massachusetts in 1634 that banned the custom of drinking to another's health, a practice that was deemed an "abominable . . . useless ceremony." (The law, largely ignored, was repealed in 1645.) In England, a small legion of moralists, politicians, and religious leaders opposed toasting and its attendant evils. In Ireland, the bishop of Cork became so upset with the practice of drinking to the dead that he issued both a stern injunction and a widely distributed pamphlet against it in 1713. Typical of the attacks on the custom is this injection from Lord Chief Justice Sir Matthew Hale, which was written for his grandchildren.

> I will not have you begin, or pledge any health, for it is become one of the greatest artifices of drinking and occasions of quarrelling in the Kingdom. If you pledge another, and a third, and so onward; and if you pledge as many as will be drank, you must be debauched and drunk. If they will needs know the reason for your refusal, it is fair to answer: "That your grandfather, who brought you up, from whom, under God, you have the estate you enjoy or expect, left this in command with you, that you should never begin or pledge a health."

Of all the crusaders against toasting, however, it would be hard to find one with a greater antagonism than William Prynne who, among other things, devoted a whole book to the link between the devil and the custom. *Healthes: Sicknesse*, published in 1628, alleges that "the great, Deuill-god Jupiter was the first inventor, founder, and institutor of our Hellish and Heathenish Healthes." It asserts that "this drinking and quaffing of healthes had its origin and birth from Pagans, heathens, and infidels, yea, from the very Deuill himself; that it is but a worldly, carnall, prophane, nay, heathenish and deuillish custom, which sauors of nothing else but Paganisme."

Prynne was certainly true to his convictions and not one to backslide at a party. On June 6, 1664, as recorded in his diary, Samuel Pepys attended a dinner at which Prynne "would not drink any health, no, not the King's but sat down with his hat on all the while; but nobody took notice of him at all."

Prynne is hardly alone in his antitoast writing. Starting with St. Augustine ("this filthy and unhappy custom of drinking healths") and continuing through the beginning of this century, a great body of literature has been amassed against the custom. In fact, The most thorough book on the subject, French's *History of Toasting*, was written by a man who despised toasting. Though scrupulously factual, French delighted in bringing to light gruesome, bloody episodes in which toasting took place. He outdid himself in describing an ancient Danish ballad:

> In one very old one, a husband after treacherously murdering his wife's twelve brothers during their sleep, and whilst they were his guests, fills a cup with their blood, which he brings to his wife that she might pledge him in it. Many years after, the wife, in retaliation, whilst her husband's relations are visiting him, steals out of bed at dead of night, murders them all, fills a cup with their gore, returns to her husband's chamber, and whilst he still sleeps securely, ties him hand and foot. She then wakes him, and after mockingly asking him to pledge her in the cup of blood, dispatches him. At that moment their baby in its cradle wakes up and cries out, so the mother, fearing lest in afterlife her son should avenge his father's murder, makes matters safe by quietly dashing its brains out.

French also uncovered such things as an ancient tribe, "the old Guebres," who exposed the corpses of their parents to the "fowls of the air," then reserved only the skulls from the decay and fashioned cups from them.

Such skullduggery notwithstanding, there were those who promoted toasting as a blessing, as an amenity and a graceful custom with, as one Victorian writer put it, "a quality as pleasant as a handshake, as warm as a kiss."

An early—if not the earliest—book entirely devoted to toasts and toasting is J. Roach's *The Royal Toastmaster*, published in London in 1791. Roach was clearly intent on cleaning up the custom's image. "Its use," he wrote of the toast, "is well known to all ranks, as a stimulative to hilarity, and an incentive to innocent mirth, to loyal truth, to pure morality and to mutual affection." At one point he ascribed great power to it:

> A Toast or Sentiment very frequently excites good humor, and revives languid conversation; often does it, when properly applied, cool the heat of resentment, and blunt the edge of animosity. A well-applied Toast is acknowledged, universally, to sooth the flame of acrimony, when season and reason oft used their efforts to no purpose.

Roach lamented "former times" and, to some extent, the "contemporary custom" of banning women from toasting sessions. In introducing his book of "decent toasts," he pointed out that the reason women were often excluded was the indecency of many toasts and the general climate of "boisterous and illiberal mirth."

If nothing else, Roach helped to set a new tone. His toasts were predictably proper ("Confusion to the minions of vice!" and "May reason be the pilot when passion blows the gale!") and politically liberal in the modern sense ("To the abolition of the slave trade," "The rights of man!" and, incredibly for 1791 England, "The liberty of North America!").

Another early collection of toasts is *The Toastmaster's Guide*, by T. Hughes, which was published in London in 1806. Like Roach, Hughes favored the quick one-liners popular at the time; but unlike Roach, he was not above including a little early-nineteenth-century spice in his toasts. A sampling from Hughes's collection:

> The two that makes a third.
> The rose of pleasure without the thorn.
> The modest maid, who covered herself with her lover.
> The commodity most thought of and least talk'd of.
> Mirth, wine and love.
> May the works of our nights never fear the day-light.
> Old wine and young women.
> Prudence and temperance with claret and champagne.
> Love without fear, and life without care.

May we never want a friend to cheer us, or a bottle to cheer
    him.
A generous heart and a miser's fortune.
Short shoes and long corns to the enemies of Great Britain.
May we do as we would be done by.
May we live in pleasure and die out of debt.
A blush of detection to the lovers of deceit.
May British cuckolds never want horns.

Many short toasts that are still heard today—"Good luck until we are tired of it!" "May poverty be a day's march behind us!" "Champagne to our real friends and real pain to our sham friends!"—appear in Hughes's book.

In the United States, the Revolutionary War and the birth of the nation were great inspirations for toasts. During the war the toasts tended in the direction of curses:

To the enemies of our country! May they have cobweb breeches,
a porcupine saddle, a hard-trotting horse, and an eternal journey.

After the war, no official dinner or celebration was complete without thirteen toasts, one for each state. The origin of the thirteen toasts may actually date from a series of banquets held in honor of George Washington on his retirement. (At one such banquet in Annapolis, Washington added a fourteenth of his own: "Sufficient Powers to Congress for general purposes!") For many years afterward, thirteen toasts were obligatory at local Fourth of July celebrations, and each toast was often followed by an artillery salute, three cheers from the crowd, and a song.

Although the Independence Day toasts differed from locale to locale, they were generally always patriotic, proud, and nonpartisan. They were dedicated to things such as the holiday itself ("May it ever be held in grateful remembrance by the American people") and the nation's presidents ("In the evenings of well-spent lives pleased with the fruits of their labors, they cheerfully await the summons that shall waft them to brighter abodes"). Invariably, there was a toast to the signers of the Declaration of Independence:

From this act of treason against the British Crown sprang a chart of Liberty and Emancipation broad as the universe and filled with glad tiding and a good will towards men. They who perilled their lives by this noble act will live and be cherished in the hearts of free men.

Though the custom of making thirteen toasts has been all but forgotten, it was recently revived at the Genesee Country Museum in Mumford, New York, as part of the local Fourth of July observation.

In the United States, toasting was enhanced by the oratorical skill of its various practitioners, including some of America's early leaders. Benjamin Franklin was among the best—if not *the* best. His most recalled toast is the one delivered at Versailles while he was the American emissary to France. On this occasion the toasting was led by the British ambassador, who said, "George III, who, like the sun in its meridian, spreads a luster throughout and enlightens the world." The next toast came from the French minister, who said, "The illustrious Louis XVI, who, like the moon, sheds his mild and benevolent rays on and influences the globe." Franklin finished the round: "George Washington, commander of the American armies, who, like Joshua of old, commanded the sun and the moon to stand still, and both obeyed."

Other influences were at work in the transfer of the custom to America. Around 1800 there was a high-spirited drinking club in London known as the Anacreontic Society, which met at the Crown and Anchor tavern. It was named for the Greek poet Anacreon, who was known for poems praising love and wine. Each meeting opened with the singing of the toast "To Anacreon in Heaven," which ended with these joyous lines:

> While thus we agree,
> Our toast let it be.
> May our club flourish happy, united and free!
> And long may the sons of Anacreon entwine,
> The myrtle of Venus with Bacchus's vine!

The composition became popular enough that a number of Americans learned it and on several occasions used the tune to accommodate their own lyrics. One of these writers was Francis Scott Key, who found it to be the perfect vehicle for his "Star-Spangled Banner."

In the decades leading up to the Civil War, many American toasts addressed the issue of union or succession. The most important of these may have been a toast delivered by President Andrew Jackson at a Jefferson Day dinner on April 13, 1830:

> Our Union: It must be preserved.

If there was a golden age for toasting, it was the period from approximately 1876—the time of the centennial—to 1920, when books and pamphlets on toasting came on the market, prominent authors contributed their own toasts to anthologies, newspapers ran columns of them, and one periodical, the *National Magazine*, actually had its own "toast editor," whose duties included judging the winners of its monthly toasting contest. Several writers of the period, such as Fred Emerson Brooks and Minna Thomas Antrim, built considerable reputations as toast writers, and the great comic poets of the time, like Oliver Herford and Wallace Irvin, created dozens of marvelous invitations to drink. One of Herford's many champagne toasts: "The bubble winked at me and said, 'You'll miss me, brother, when you're dead.'"

Toasts were written for every imaginable institution, situation, and type of person—cities, colleges, states, holidays, baseball teams, fools, failures, short people, and fat people. A British collection contained a toast, several pages in length, written for "The Opening of an Electric Generating Station." Occupational toasts were very popular, and some clubs and fraternal organizations opened their dinners with a toast to each of the professions represented at the table. Many of these incorporated at least one atrocious pun:

> **The Grocer:** Whose honest tea is the best policy!
> **The Paper Hanger:** Who is always up against it and still remains stuck up!
> **The Conductor:** May he always know what is fare!
> **The Author:** The queerest of animals; their tales come out of their heads!

The Baker: Who loafs around all day and still makes the dough!

The Glazier: Who takes panes to see his way through life!

The Well-Digger: Always feel above your business, and be glad of the fact that you do not have to begin at the bottom and work to the top!

Undertakers: May they never overtake us!

Blacksmiths: Success to forgery!

Painters: When we work in the wet, may we never want for dryers.

And the humble shoemaker was blessed with a host of toasts: He's a stick to the last . . . He left his awl . . . He pegged out . . . He was well heeled, but lost his sole . . . He was on his uppers.

This was also a time for more elaborate toasts; the long, florid, and overblown ones no doubt put many to sleep. Some of these toast-essays, however, had punch, such as the one that took first prize in a 1911 *National Magazine* contest. The toast, titled "The Way of a Woman," was submitted by Miss Saidee Lewis and went on for many lines, concluding with this paragraph:

Of those marriageable misses, thinking life all love and kisses, mist and moonshine, glint and glamour, Stardust borrowed from the skies! Man's a gross and sordid lummox—men are largely made of stomachs, and the songs of all the sirens will not take the place of pies!

Political and military toasts could reach near epic proportions. An anti–Teddy Roosevelt toast, "No! Teddy Don't Play Fair," drones on for eleven stanzas before it gets to the point:

But honest old Bill Bryan,
With kindliness will wear
Away all Republican lyin'
No! Teddy don't play fair.

Ironically, a number of toasts were written in honor of the teeto-taler Bryan, who himself once was called on to toast the British navy. He lifted his glass of water and said, "Gentlemen, I believe your victories were won on water."

A toast written in honor of Alton B. Parker after his unsuccessful bid for the presidency in 1904 is also typical of the period—if nothing else, it rhymes:

It's a pardonable pride a Democrat feels
For Alton B. Parker, Court of Appeals,
He bore our standard last campaign,
And although his fight was in vain,
Alton B. Parker, you're alright.
Alton B. Parker, may your skies be bright.

When prohibition went into effect in 1920, the drinking continued, but the customs changed. A writer who was trying to reintroduce toasting and other traditional drinking customs in 1934 after the law was repealed put it this way: "When Prohibition placed its stranglehold on our nation, it doomed for more than thirteen years the real art and etiquette of drinking."

On the banned list were not only wine, beer, and spirits, but, for all practical purposes, the formularies, books, ads, and magazine articles that helped carry the lore and customs of drinking. A good bootlegger could get a few bottles of champagne (or a reasonable facsimile) for a wedding, but no publishers were printing collections of new wedding toasts. Banquets, parties, and other functions where one used to have a drink or two and launch a few toasts were now scarce and usually dry. Places where one would go for a leisurely drink to toast the health of a friend's new baby—the corner saloon, the cocktail lounge, and the hotel bar—were shut down and replaced by dank speakeasies where one would slink to have a fast drink of questionable origin.

This is not to say that people did not toast, but in many cases their toasts' substance had to do with the Volstead Act, the antisaloonists, and the quality of bathtub gin. For example:

Here's to prohibition,
The devil take it!
They've stolen our wine,
So now we make it.

The moment prohibition was repealed, there was a lot of toasting—which, for the most part, was addressed to the act itself. But after this initial flurry, the custom of the toast continued to decline. Of course, many upheld the tradition, and from time to time new toasts appeared, such as these two examples from the 1930s and 1950s, respectively:

Here's to the new radio—
Here's to our neighbor's loudspeaker
So loud we need none of our own
May its volume never grow weaker.

Here's to today!
For tomorrow we may be radioactive.

Fortunately, a few advocates of toasting have helped to preserve and perpetuate the custom. Like those who carried the seeds of the Renaissance through the Dark Ages, and like others who have gone against the cultural tide, they are

THE MCELVY LEGACY: When New Yorker Douglas McElvy passed away in 1973, he left twelve thousand dollars for friends to toast him on the anniversary of his death. The cash lasted for three years, but, according to reports in the papers, his friends still meet each New Year's Day at the bar where the legacy was drained to pour him a memorial gin and tonic and toast his empty stool.

THE COSGROVIANS: A society of self-styled bons vivants who for some years assembled each month in Washington, D.C., to honor the memory of an ardent prohibitionist named Cosgrove who left water-dispensing monuments to the abstemious spirit. The Cosgrovian's toast: "Temperance. I'll drink to that!"

THE MCGOWAN INFLUENCE: If there is one place in the world today where the custom is doing well, it is Ireland. Jack McGowan, an affable man with the sponsorship of the Irish Distillers International in Dublin, has collected toasts and Irish blessings over the years. He shares this treasury with interested parties in so-called civilized areas of the world where the custom is presently out of style. Toasts from McGowan's collection have shown up in American newspaper columns and form the bulk of the Irish toasts section of this book.

SUMMIT TALK: Then there is the business of glasnost and the changing relationship between the United States and the Soviet Union. This thawing and warming was accompanied by so much toasting that the *Washington Post*'s headline the morning after the historic June 1990 Gorbachev-Bush dinner at the Soviet embassy in Washington was TOASTED INSIDE AND OUT AT THE SOVIET EMBASSY. These toasts actually featured a degree of levity, such as George H. W. Bush's reference to the two leaders' previous meetings anchored off the coast of the island nation of Malta: "[To] the memories of the days we spent in Malta—friendship, cooperation, seasick pills . . ."

MASS TOASTING: On April 11, 2009, at 7 P.M. at over six thousand venues across the United Kingdom, there was a bid to break the world record for the largest toast in history as part of "National Cask Ale Week." The previous record stood at 485,000 people. But because of the ability of Facebook and Twitter to spread the word quickly, the event spread to pubs in other countries, including Australia and the United States. As of this writing, the complex job of counting and verifying the final number was still under way, but it is almost certain that a new record has been established and—given the ever-increasing power of the Internet—that new attempts will be made to set new toasting records. This event competes with another, held annually on the third Friday in February and sometimes known as "St. Practice Day," made up of Guinness drinkers across the world who are also after trying to break the record for the largest simultaneous toast. The battle lines have been drawn.

The Art of Toasting

1. BE PREPARED AND KEEP THE TOAST SHORT. If you aren't prepared, you are most likely to speak for too long. Think the toast through, write it down, and practice saying it aloud once or twice. Mark Twain said that no toast—other than the ones he gave—should last for more than one minute. So, no more than a minute. Most toasts should not exceed thirty seconds.

A good example is the toast Senator Dianne Feinstein gave to President Barack Obama moments after he was elected:

> And now I would like to propose a toast to the new president of the United States. Mr. President, Mrs. Obama, so much rests on your shoulders: our hopes, our dreams, the future of this country. We've watched you. We see the equanimity. We see the dedication. We see the balance. And I think the sense of all of us in this room is that this nation is in good hands. May those hands remain stable and steady. May those hands always be well. May you and your family be blessed with the love of the American people. And may we in government be your partner in the future of this great country.
>
> We salute you, Mr. President.

This toast—by all accounts, the most witnessed toast in human history—fulfilled its purpose in less than thirty seconds and exactly 113 words—neither too long nor too short.

The fact that the guests will be holding their glasses aloft is another reason for brevity, and relative sobriety. You don't want to be known as the best man or other functionary who tippled too much champagne and gave a rambling toast while the other guests' arms fell asleep under the strain of full glasses.

The challenge is that brevity requires work—rambling requires none. Flubbing the toast is like serving stale champagne: it flattens the mood. If you need to read the toast from a piece of paper, then ask for the other guests' indulgence by saying something like "I wrote this down because I don't want to miss a single word and it is important that I get it right."

2. BE KIND AND SINCERE, AND DON'T TRY TO BE FUNNY IF YOU ARE NOT. *Sincerity* and *preparation* are the two key words. Quote Shakespeare, quote from the Bible or other sources, but give the words and their relation to the person toasted or the occasion some thought.

"One mistake people make at weddings and big events is they try to be funny. If you're going to try and be funny, please, please, please, on behalf of all the people sitting in the audience, test your material in advance on someone who won't lie to you or give you token laughs," Renate Zorn, a coordinator for the Toastmasters Speakers Bureau, told the *Toronto Star* in a September 2004 article on toasting. "It's for your own good: Anyone who has told a joke to a couple of hundred people and bombed knows that's not an experience worth trying twice. And if you can't make one person laugh with a line, I guarantee you're not getting a roomful to even crack a smile."

3. THINK OF YOUR TOAST AS AN IMPORTANT VERBAL SOUVENIR. People remember a really good—or a really bad—toast long after the event at which it was delivered. The toast should elevate the mood of the room one notch higher, and give everyone a sense of commonality. This is especially true for wedding toasts, but also for other important occasions from baptisms to retirement parties. People often spend hours shopping for a tux or a gown, but neglect to spend any time composing a toast, which is an important souvenir of the day.

4. STAND (OR SIT) AND DELIVER. If possible, stand when you are delivering a toast. If you are uncomfortable standing, or unable to stand, it is acceptable to remain seated. Hold the glass at shoulder-level in your right hand. Speak clearly and confidently. Speak loudly and clearly so everyone can hear you and understand your words. Briefly introduce yourself before the toast if you aren't already known by everyone present.

5. END UP. Always end your toast on a positive note and alert the guests to join in. For example, say "Cheers!" or ask the audience to "Raise your glass."

6. CLINK BEFORE YOU DRINK. Clink—but do not clunk—your glass after the toast is given but before it's drunk. One story links the clinking of glasses to an old belief that the devil is frightened away by bells—church bells and others. This protective gesture still has a nice ring to it.

7. NEVERS

NEVER refuse to participate in a toast. It is better to toast with an empty glass than not at all.

NEVER use a toast to complain or advance a personal agenda—it ain't about you.

NEVER hit your glass with a spoon—it is disharmonious and can destroy good stemware.

NEVER exclude anyone because they do not have a full glass, and always make sure that minors and nondrinkers are provided for. Don't cut out a nine-year-old from a wedding toast because somebody forgot the ginger ale. A toast is the ultimate act of inclusion, so make sure no one is left out.

NEVER bring up ex-wives, old boyfriends, academic failure, or inside jokes that no one else will understand, or try to turn these into something funny.

And NEVER, NEVER confuse a toast with a practical joke. The best man's toast is not a good time for practical joking. Alan Feldman, of Feldman's Photography in Brandon, Florida, has seen that go awry. As he told a *Tampa Tribune* reporter for a 1996 article on toasting disasters, he worked at a wedding in which the best man passed out keys to about thirty women. When the best man raised his glass to toast the newlyweds, he announced that it was time for all the women who were having affairs with the groom to return his house keys. The multitudes walked up and dropped the keys in front of the bride.

"She was so upset; it ruined the rest of the wedding," Feldman said. "No doubt the honeymoon was heavy on the chill and light on the bubbly." Feldman says the bride did not talk to the groom—presumably because he chose such a best man—for the rest of the reception.

8. RULE FOR THE TOASTEE: Respond to the toast appropriately. The toastee (the person being toasted) should not stand or drink to him- or herself. Once the toast is finished, you may bow or offer thanks in acknowledgment. You may also raise your own glass to propose a toast to the host, the toaster, or anyone else.

How to Use This Book

THIS BOOK HAS been designed for quick access as well as leisurely browsing. To accomplish both of these ends, all the toasting topics, and the toasts gathered under those topics, have been alphabetized. Anyone looking for "Hints for Effective Toasting," a collection of historic toasts, or toasts having to with health, home, or husbands will be rewarded by looking under *H*. *L* yields toasts about love, luck, and lust, in that order—a good toast right there.

The table of contents and the generous use of cross-references to similar categories (look for "see also" at the end of a section) conspire to help you find appropriate toasts quickly, which in turn should make you rich, famous, and popular beyond your wildest dreams.

Toasts and Toasting

AGE

A man is only as old as the woman he feels.
—GROUCHO MARX

Do not resist growing old—many are denied the privilege.

Fill high the goblet! Envious time steals, as we speak, our fleeting prime.

Here's a health to the future;
    A sigh for the past;
We can love and remember,
    And hope to the last,
And for all the base lies
    That the almanacs hold
While there's love in the heart,
    We can never grow old.

Here's hoping that you live forever
And mine is the last voice you hear.
—WILLARD SCOTT, from *A Gentleman's Guide to Toasting*

Here's that we may live to eat the hen
That scratches on our grave.

I've never known a person to live to 110 or more, and then die, to be remarkable for anything else.
—Josh Billings

Let him live to be a hundred! We want him on earth.
—Oliver Wendell Holmes to a friend

Long life to you and may you die in your own bed.

May our lives, like the leaves of the maple, grow
    More beautiful as they fade.
May we say our farewells, when it's time to go,
    All smiling and unafraid.
—Larry E. Johnson

May the Lord love us but not call us too soon.

May virtue and truth
Guide you in youth
Catnip and sage
Cheer your old age.
—Found in a geography book dated 1880, Cuttingsville, Vermont

May we keep a little of the fuel of youth to warm our body in old age.

May you enter heaven late.

May you live as long as you want, may you never want as long as you live.

May you live to be a hundred—and decide the rest for yourself.

Noah was six hundred years old before he knew how to build an ark—don't lose your grip.
—Elbert Hubbard

Oh to be seventy again!
—OLIVER WENDELL HOLMES JR. on the occasion of his passing a
    pretty girl on the street at the age of about eighty-five

Only the young die good.
—OLIVER HERFORD

The good die young—here's hoping that you may live to a ripe
old age.

To maturity:
    When there's snow on the roof,
    there's fire in the furnace.

To the Old Guard, the older we grow,
The more we take and the less we know.
At least the young men tell us so,
But the day will come, when they shall know
Exactly how far a glass can go,
To win the battle, 'gainst age, the foe.
Here's youth . . . in a glass of wine.
—JAMES MONROE MCLEAN, *The Book of Wine*

To the old, long life and treasure;
To the young, all health and pleasure.
—BEN JONSON

You're not as young as you used to be
But you're not as old as you're going to be
So watch it!
—Irish

SEE ALSO: *Birthdays; Health; New Year's*

ALLITERATIVE

Here's an alphabetical selection of this long-popular toast form. Many of these were regarded as old at the time of the American Revolution. Included at the end are two toast oddities in one: an orderly Jacobite offering and an acrostic.

Abundance, abstinence, and annihilation.
Abundance to the poor,
Abstinence to the intemperate,
Annihilation to the wicked.

Bachelors, banns, and buns.
Bachelors for the maidens,
Banns* for the bachelors,
Buns after the consummation of the banns.

Cheerfulness, content, and competency.
Cheerfulness in our cups,
Content in our minds,
Competency in our pockets.

The three good C's: conscience, claret, and cash.

Firmness, freedom, and fortitude.
Firmness in the Senate,
Freedom on the land,
Fortitude on the waves.

Friendship, feeling, and fidelity.
Friendship without interest,
Feeling to our enemies,
Fidelity to our friends.

---

* Banns: the stated intention to marry.

The three H's: health, honor, and happiness.
Health to all the world,
Honor to those who seek for it,
Happiness in our homes.

The eight H's:
Handsome Husband,
Handsome House,
Health and Happiness,
Here and Hereafter.

Love, life, and liberty.
Love pure,
Life long,
Liberty boundless.

Mirth, music, and moderation.
Mirth at every board,
Music in all instruments,
Moderation in our desires.

Wine, wit, and wisdom.
Wine enough to sharpen wit,
Wit enough to give zest to wine,
Wisdom enough to "shut down" at the right time.

The following, known as the Jacobite Toast, is ascribed to Lord Duff, who presented it in the year 1745.

A	B	C		A Blessed Change.
D	E	F		Down Every Foreigner.
G	H	J		Good Help James.
K	L	M		Keep Lord Marr.
N	O	P		Noble Ormond Preserve.
Q	R	S		Quickly Resolve Stewart.
T	U	V	W	Truss Up Vile Whigs.
X	Y	Z		'Xert Your Zeal.

AMERICA

Legend has it that sometime during the middle of the last century, three Americans were called on to toast their country at a dinner party in Paris. All were duly impressed with the size and growing importance of their country, and each tried to top the other in expressing his feelings. Here is the result:

1. Here's to the United States—bounded on the north by British America, on the south by the Gulf of Mexico, on the east by the Atlantic Ocean, and the west by the Pacific Ocean!

2. Here's to the United States—bounded on the north by the North Pole, on the south by the South Pole, on the east by the rising sun, and on the west by the setting sun.

3. I give you the United States—bounded on the north by the Aurora Borealis, on the south by the procession of the equinoxes, on the east by primeval chaos, and on the west by the Day of Judgment!

Other American toasts from various eras:

A toast before we go:
Huzzah for America, ho!
Let us care for no man,
If no man cares for us.

America and England: and may they never have any division but the Atlantic between them.
—CHARLES DICKENS

America—half-brother of the world!—
with something good and bad of every land.
—PHILIP BAYLEY

Here's to Columbia, free laws and a free church,
From their blessings may plotters be left in the lurch;
Give us pure candidates and a pure ballot box,
And our freedom shall stand as firm as the rocks.

Here's to the memory
Of the man
That raised the corn
That fed the goose
That bore the quill
That made the pen
That wrote the Declaration of Independence.

It is my loving sentiment, and by the blessing of God it shall be
my dying sentiment—Independence now and Independence
forever!
—Daniel Webster

Let us ever remember that our interest is in concord, not in conflict;
and that our real eminence rests in the victories of peace, not those
of war.
—William McKinley, at the Pan-American Exposition,
    September 5, 1901

May the enemies of America be destitute of beef and claret.

May the liberties of America never be clipped by the shears of bad
economy.

May the world's wonder be American thunder.
—The three eighteenth-century toasts above come from an extremely early
    American toast book located in the rare book collection of the Library of
    Congress. The book, *Everybody's Toast Book*, is undated but clearly comes
    from the late eighteenth or very early nineteenth century.

One flag, one land, one heart, one hand, one nation evermore.
—Oliver Wendell Holmes

Our country, Congress, cash, and courage.

Our country! In her intercourse with foreign nations, may she always
be in the right; but our country right or wrong.
—STEPHEN DECATUR

Our country! When right, to be kept right. When wrong, to be put right!
—CARL SCHURZ, who was doubtlessly responding to the statement by
Decatur, which was a very popular toast for many years and which became
a rallying cry for supporters of U.S. government policies during the
Vietnam War

To America: With all its faults and blemishes, this country gives a
man elbowroom to do what is nearest his heart.
—ERIC HOPPER, *First Things, Last Things*

To her we drink, for her we pray,
Our voices silent never;
For her we'll fight, come what come may,
The Stars and Stripes forever!

To its laughter, to its tears,
To the hope that after-years
Find us plodding on the way
Without so much tax to pay.

To our country! Lift your glasses!
To its sun-capped mountain passes,
To its forest, its streams,
To its memories, its dreams.

To Uncle Sam:

Addition to his friends,
Subtraction from his wants,
Multiplication of his blessings,
Division among his foes.

SEE ALSO: *Historic; Military*

37

ANNIVERSARIES

Here is to loving, to romance, to us.
May we travel together through time.
We alone count as none, but together we're one,
For our partnership puts love to rhyme.
—Irish

Here's to you both—
a beautiful pair,
on the birthday
of your love affair.

Let anniversaries come and let anniversaries go—but may your
happiness continue on forever.

Love seems the swiftest, but it is
the slowest of growths. No man
or woman really knows what
perfect love is until they have
been married a quarter of a
century.
—MARK TWAIN

May the warmth of our
affections survive the frosts of age.

To your coming anniversaries—
may they be outnumbered only by your coming pleasures.

We've holidays and holy days, and memory days galore;
And when we've toasted every one, I offer just one more.
So let us lift our glasses high, and drink a silent toast—
The day, deep buried in each heart, that each one loves the most.

Wine comes in at the mouth
    And love comes in at the eye;
That's all that we will know for truth
    Before we grow old and die.
I lift the glass to my mouth,
    I look at you and I sigh.
—WILLIAM BUTLER YEATS

With fifty years between you
    and your well-kept wedding vow.
The Golden Age, old friends of mine,
    is not a fable now.
—JOHN GREENLEAF WHITTIER, "The Golden Wedding at Longwood"

SEE ALSO: *Weddings*

APRIL FOOLS' DAY

April 1. This is the day upon which we are reminded of what we are on the other three hundred and sixty-four.
—MARK TWAIN, *Pudd'nhead Wilson*, 1894

April fool, n. The March fool with another month added to his folly.
—AMBROSE BIERCE, *The Devil's Dictionary*

Even the gods love jokes.
—PLATO

It is the ability to take a joke, not make one, that proves you have a sense of humor.
—MAX EASTMAN

Let us toast the fools. But for them the rest of us could not succeed.
—MARK TWAIN

Lord, what fools these mortals be.
—WILLIAM SHAKESPEARE, *A Midsummer Night's Dream*, Act III

Take all the fools out of this world and there wouldn't be any fun living in it, or profit.
—JOSH BILLINGS

The trouble with practical jokes is that very often they get elected.
—WILL ROGERS

BABIES AND CHILDREN

A baby will make love stronger, days shorter, nights longer, bankroll smaller, home happier, clothes shabbier, the past forgotten, and the future worth living for.

A generation of children on the children of your children.

A lovely being scarcely formed or molded,
A rose with all its sweetest leaves yet folded.
—LORD BYRON

A new life begun,
Like father, like son.
—Irish

Every baby born into the world is a finer one than the last.
—CHARLES DICKENS, *Nicholas Nickleby*

Father of fathers, make me one,
A fit example for a son.
—DOUGLAS MALLOCH, toast for fathers with a son or sons

Grandchildren are gifts of God.
It is God's way . . .
Of compensating us for growing
      old.
—Irish

Here's to the baby—man to be—
May he be as fine as thee!
Here's to baby—woman to be—
May she be as sweet as thee!

Here's to the stork,
A most valuable bird,
That inhabits the residence districts.
He doesn't sing tunes,
Nor yield any plumes,
But he helps the vital statistics.
—Irish

Like one, like the other,
Like daughter, like mother.
—Irish

May he/she grow twice as tall as yourself and half as wise.
—Irish

Out of a love our child will grow . . .
Greater than light, deeper than dark,
All other love is but a spark.

So that our children will have wealthy parents.

The Babies. —As they comfort us in our sorrows, let us not forget
them in our festivities
—MARK TWAIN

"The stork has brought a little peach!"
The nurse said with an air.
"I'm mighty glad," the father said.
"He didn't bring a pear."

Trust yourself. You know more than you think you do.
—BENJAMIN SPOCK, psychologist, advice to a new parent in
 Baby and Child Care, 1977

We haven't all the good fortune to be ladies; we have not all been
generals, or poets or statesmen; but when the toast works down to the
babies we stand on common ground. We've all been babies.
—MARK TWAIN

SEE ALSO: *Parents*

BEER AND ALE

Ale's a strong wrestler,
Flings all it hath met;
And makes the ground slippery,
Though it not be wet.

Beer! Beer! Beer!
We students do adore you,
Beer! Beer! Beer!
We love to see you foam;
When we for wine abjure you,
We miss you we assure you,
For it's only with clear sparkling beer
That students feel at home.

Champagne costs too much,
Whiskey's too rough,
Vodka puts big mouths in gear.
This little refrain
Should help to explain
Why it's better to order a beer!

Come, sit we by the fireside
And roundly drink we hear,
Till that we see our cheeks all dyed
And noses tanned with beer.
—ROBERT HERRICK

Fill with mingled cream and amber,
I will drain that glass again.
Such hilarious visions clamber
Through the chamber of my brain.
Quaintest thoughts, queerest fancies
Come to life and fade away.
What care I how time advances;
I am drinking ale today.
—EDGAR ALLAN POE

Good pies and strong beer.
—*Poor Robin's Almanack*, 1695

He that buys land buys many stones.
He that buys flesh buys many bones.
He that buys eggs buys many shells,
But he that buys good beer buys nothing else.

Here's to the best ale in the best ale.
—MR. PICKWICK, in Charles Dickens's *Pickwick Papers*

In heaven there is no beer . . .
That's why we drink ours here.
—Anonymous

"Let No Man Thirst for Lack of Real Ale."
—Matchbook toast from the Commonwealth Brewing Co.,
  Boston, Massachusetts

Let's drink the liquid of amber so bright;
Let's drink the liquid with foam snowy white;
Let's drink the liquid that brings all good cheer;
Oh, where is the drink like old-fashioned beer?
—A popular nineteenth-century toast often adapted to the use of a
  particular brand whose name was substituted for "old-fashioned"
  in the last line

None so deaf as those who will not hear.
None so blind as those who will not see.
But I'll wager none so deaf nor blind that he
Sees not nor hears me say come drink this beer.
—W. L. Hassoldt

Show me a nation whose national beverage is beer, and I'll show you
an advanced toilet technology.
—Mark Hawkins, in the New
  York Times, September 25, 1977

Thirsty days hath September,
April, June and November;
All the rest are thirsty too
Except for him who hath
        home brew.
—Realbeer.com

Who'd care to be a bee and sip
Sweet honey from the flower's lip
When he might be a fly and steer
Headfirst into a can of beer?

Why, we'll smoke and drink our beer.
For I like a drop of good beer, I does.
I'ze fond of good beer, I is.
Let gentlemen fine sit down to their wine.
But we'll all of us here stick to our beer.
—Somersetshire drinking song

You foam within our glasses, you lusty golden brew,
Whoever imbibes takes fire from you.
The young and the old sing your praises,
Here's to beer,
Here's to cheer,
Here's to beer!
—From the opera *The Bartered Bride*

SEE ALSO: *Libations; Revelry; Spirits (Ardent)*

BETTER TIMES

A speedy calm to the storms of life.

All of this has been a religious experience: a living hell.

Bury the blue devils.*

---

* The original version is longer:

  Come fill the bowl, each jolly soul;
  Let Bacchus guide our revels;
  Join cup to lip, with "hip, hip, hip,"
  And bury the blue devils.

Everybody in life gets the same amount of ice. The rich get it in the summer and the poor in the winter.
—BAT MASTERSON. These words were found in the sportswriter's typewriter after he suffered a fatal heart attack.

Here's a health to poverty; it sticks by us when our friends forsake us.

Here's to thee my honest friend,
Wishing these hard times to mend.

If the world is going wrong,
     Forget it!
Sorrow never lingers long—
     Forget it!
If your neighbor bears ill will,
If your conscience won't be still,
If you owe an ancient bill,
     Forget it!

If this is a blessing, it is certainly *very* well disguised.
—WINSTON CHURCHILL on his defeat in the 1945 general election, quoted by Richard Nixon in *Memoirs of Richard Nixon*

Laugh and the world laughs with you;
Weep, and it gives you the laugh anyway.

Let us make our glasses kiss;
Let us quench the sorrow-cinders.
—RALPH WALDO EMERSON, in *The Persian of Hafiz*, 1851

May poverty always be a day's march behind us.

May the morning of prosperity shine on the evening of adversity.

May the sunshine of comfort dispel the clouds of despair.

May we ever be able to part with our troubles to advantage.

Remember the poor—it costs nothing.
—Josh Billings

The right time and place is coming for you. Don't let it pass.
—Fortune cookie message

To the Great Unknown—who is waiting to do us a favor.

Troubles like babies grow larger by nursing.

Worry is rust upon the blade.
—Henry Ward Beecher

SEE ALSO: *General; Luck; Past, Present, and Future*

BIBLICAL

While the Bible does not directly mention toasting, a number of passages indicate that the custom was observed. Even an antitoast cleric of the last century had to concede, "It is hardly probable that Ben-hadad and the thirty-two kings, his companions, would drink themselves drunk in the pavilions without some interchange of courtesies" (see 1 Kings 20:16).

Some lines from the Bible have been used as toasts, including these:

A feast is made for laughter, and wine maketh merry.
—Ecclesiastes 10:19

Do not arouse or awaken love until it so desires.
—Song of Solomon 2:7

Drink no longer water, but use a little wine for thy stomach's sake.
—1 Timothy 5:23

Eat thy bread with joy, and drink thy wine with a merry heart.
—Ecclesiastes 9:7

Forsake not an old friend, for the new is not comparable to him. A new friend is as new wine: when it is old, thou shall drink it with pleasure.
—Ecclesiastes 9:10

Give . . . wine unto those that be of heavy heart.
—Proverbs 31:6

The best wine . . . that goeth down sweetly, causing the lips of those that are asleep to speak.
—Song of Solomon 7:9

Wine maketh glad the heart of man.
—Psalms 104:15

Wine nourishes, refreshes, and cheers. Wine is the foremost of all medicines . . . Whenever wine is lacking, medicines become necessary.
—The Talmud

Wine was created from the beginning to make men joyful, and not to make men drunk. Wine drunk with moderation is the joy of the soul and the heart.
—Ecclesiastes 31:35–36

Wine, which cheereth God and man.
—Judges 9:13

SEE ALSO: *Food*

BIRTHDAYS

A health, and many of them. Birthdays were never like this when
I had 'em.

Although another year is past
He's/She's no older than the last!

Another candle on your cake?
Well, that's no cause to pout,
Be glad that you have strength
    enough
To blow the damn thing out.

Another year older? Think this way:
Just one day older than yesterday!

God grant you many and happy years,
    Till, when the last has crowned you,
The dawn of endless days appears,
    And heaven is shining round you!
—OLIVER WENDELL HOLMES

Happy birthday to you
    And many to be,
With friends that are true
    As you are to me!

Here's to you! No matter how old you are, you don't look it!

Many happy returns of the day of your birth:
Many blessings to brighten your pathway on earth;
Many friendships to cheer and provoke you to mirth;
Many feastings and frolics to add to your girth.
—ROBERT H. LORD

May you have been born on your lucky star and may that star never lose its twinkle.

May you live to be a hundred years with one extra year to repent.
—Irish

Time marches on!
Now tell the truth—
Where did you find
The fountain of youth?

To wish you joy on your birthday
And all the whole year through,
For all the best that life can hold
Is none too good for you.

To your birthday, glass held high,
Glad it's you that's older—not I.

SEE ALSO: *Age; Health*

BULLS

This term for absurd contradictions—e.g., "It's a mighty good thing for your wife that you're not married"—goes back at least to the thirteenth century. Some have become toasts:

A toast to posterity—though it does nothing for us.

Here's to _____, equal to none.

Here's to abstinence—as long as it's practiced in moderation.

Here's to the glorious _____, the last in the fight and the first out.

Here's to your wedding and many of them.

I hope you are all here to do honor to the toast. As many of ye as is present will say "Here!" and as many of ye as is not present will say "Absent!"

Liberty all over the world, and everywhere else.

May every patriot love his native country, whether he was born in it or not.

To our health. May it remain with us long after we die.

CELIA'S TOAST (WITH VARIATIONS)

Drink to me only with thine eyes,
    And I will pledge with mine;
Or leave a kiss but in the cup,
    And I'll not look for wine.
—BEN JONSON, "To Celia"

Drink to me only with thine eyes,
    And I will pledge with mine;
For I would have to pledge my watch
    If she should drink more wine.

Drink to me only with thine eyes,
    And I will pledge with mine;
Or, leave a kiss within the cup—
    I'll wash it down with wine.

Drink to me only with thine eyes?
I'll take a little wine.
    The eyes we prize
    Are full of lies,
I'll none of that in mine.

CHAMPAGNE

In the classic film *All About Eve* there is a scene when Bette Davis's character, Margo, and pals are having dinner in the Cub Room and Hugh Marlowe's character, Lloyd, observes: "For some reason you just can't pick up champagne and drink it. Someone has to be very witty about a toast." Here are some possibilities for such an occasion.

Here's champagne to our real friends and real pain to our sham friends.

Here's to champagne, the drink divine,
That makes us forget all our troubles;
It's made of a dollar's worth of wine
And three dollars' worth of bubbles.*

If ever . . . in the eternal times that are to come, you and I shall sit down in Paradise, in some little shady corner by ourselves; and if we shall by any means be able to smuggle a basket of champagne there (I won't believe in a Temperance Heaven), and if we shall then cross our celestial legs in the celestial grass that is forever tropical, and strike our glasses and our heads together, till both musically ring in concert,—then, O my dear fellow-mortal, how shall we pleasantly discourse of all the things manifold which now so distress us,—when

---

* This is the original version of the toast, which is at least ninety years old, so you may want to adjust the dollar amounts for inflation.

all the earth shall be but a reminiscence, yea, its final dissolution an antiquity.

—HERMAN MELVILLE to Nathaniel Hawthorne

O thrice accursed
Be a champagne thirst,
When the price of beer's all we've got.

Some take their gold
In minted mold,
And some in harps hereafter,
But give me mine
In bubbles fine
And keep the change in laughter.

—OLIVER HERFORD

The bubble winked at me and said,
"You'll miss me, brother, when
    you're dead."

—OLIVER HERFORD

Three be the things I shall never attain: envy, content, and sufficient champagne.

—DOROTHY PARKER

To the glorious, golden vintage of France,
Whose bubbling beauties our spirits entrance;
When with friends tried and true this nectar we quaff
We wish for a neck like a thirsty giraffe.

SEE ALSO: *Libations; Revelry; Wine*

CHEESES

Cheese—milk's leap toward immortality.
—CLIFTON FADIMAN

CAMEMBERT

Soft, aromatic, ammoniacal,
Angelic half, half demoniacal;
We pledge thee, Camembert,
The Rare:
Thou apotheosis of decay.
—W. E. P. FRENCH

LIMBURGER

The rankest compound of villainous smell that ever offended
nostril.
—WILLIAM SHAKESPEARE, *The Merry Wives of Windsor*, Act III

ROQUEFORT

The king of cheeses and the cheese of kings.

CHRISTMAS

A Christmas wish—
May you never forget
what is worth remembering
or remember
what is best forgotten.
—Irish

A Merry Christmas this December
To a lot of folks I don't remember.
—FRANKLIN P. ADAMS, 1922

As fits the holy Christmas birth,
　　Be this, good friends, our carol still—
Be peace on earth, be peace on earth,
　　To men of gentle will.
—William Makepeace Thackeray

At Christmas play and make good cheer
For Christmas comes but once a year.
—Thomas Tusser

Be merry all, be merry all,
With holly dress the festive hall,
Prepare the song, the feast, the ball,
To welcome Merry Christmas.

Blessed is the season which engages the whole world in a conspiracy
of love.
—Hamilton Wright Mabie

Christmas is here,
Merry old Christmas,
Gift-bearing, heart-touching, joy-bringing Christmas,
Day of grand memories, king of the year.
—Washington Irving

Fifty more Christmases at least in this life, and eternal summers
in another.
—Charles Dickens, Mr. Pickwick's Christmas dinner toast

Heap on more wood!—the wind is chill
　　But let it whistle as it will,
We'll keep our Christmas merry still.
—Sir Walter Scott

Here's to the day of good will, cold weather, and warm hearts!

Here's to the holly with its bright red berry.
Here's to Christmas, let's make it merry.

God bless us every one!
—CHARLES DICKENS, Tiny Tim's toast in *A Christmas Carol*

Or, for those who would like to savor the entire incident:

> At last the dinner was all done, the cloth cleared, the hearth swept, and the fire made up. The compound in the jug being tasted, and considered perfect, apples and oranges were put upon the table, and a shovelful of chestnuts on the fire. Then all the Cratchit family drew around the hearth in what Bob Cratchit called a circle, meaning half a one; and at Bob Cratchit's elbow stood the family display of glass. Two tumblers and a custard-cup without a handle.
>
> These held the hot stuff from the jug, however, as well as golden goblets would have done; and Bob served it out with beaming looks, while the chestnuts on the fire sputtered and crackled noisily. Then Bob proposed:
>
> "A Merry Christmas to us all, my dears. God bless us!"
>
> Which the family re-echoed.
>
> "God bless us every one!" said Tiny Tim, the last of all.
>
> —CHARLES DICKENS, *A Christmas Carol*

Here's wishing you more happiness
Than all my words can tell,
Not just alone for Christmas
But for all the year as well.

Holly and ivy hanging up
And something wet in every cup.
—Irish

I have always thought of Christmas as a good time; a kind, forgiving, generous, pleasant time; a time when men and women seem by one

consent to open their hearts freely; and so I say "God bless Christmas."
—CHARLES DICKENS

I know I've wished you this before
But every year I wish it more,
A Merry Christmas.
—From an old postcard

I wish you a Merry Christmas
And a Happy New Year
A pocket full of money
And a cellar full of beer!

Joy to the world—and especially to you.

May the Virgin and her Child lift your latch on Christmas night.
—Irish, referring to the old Irish custom of leaving the door unbolted and a
    candle in the window for Mary on her way to Bethlehem

May you be as contented as Christmas finds you all the year round.
—Irish

May you be poor in misfortune this Christmas
and rich in blessings
slow to make enemies
quick to make friends
and rich or poor, slow or quick,
as happy as the New Year is long.
—Irish

May you be the first house in the parish to welcome St. Nicholas.
—Irish

May you live as long as you wish, and have all you wish as long as you live. This is my Christmas wish for you.

May you never be without a drop at Christmas.
—Irish

May your corn stand high as yourself, your fields grow bigger
with rain, and the mare know its own way home on Christmas
night.
—Irish

May your sheep all have lambs but not on Christmas night.
—Irish

Now, thrice welcome, Christmas!
Which brings us good cheer,
Mince pies and plum pudding,
Strong ale and strong beer!

Peace and plenty for many a Christmas to come.
—Irish

Then here's to the heartening wassail,
Wherever good fellows are found;
Be its master instead of its vassal,
And order the glasses around.
—Ogden Nash

Then let us be merry and taste the good cheer,
And remember old Christmas comes but once a year.
—From an old Christmas carol

'Twas the month after Christmas,
And Santa had flit;
Came there tidings for father
Which read: "Please remit!"

"A toast—Jedediah—to life on my terms. These are the only terms anybody ever knows, his own."
—ORSON WELLES, *Citizen Kane*

"Gentlemen, I give you a toast. Here's my hope that Robert Conway will find his Shangri-La. Here's my hope that we all find our Shangri-La."
—HUGH BUCKLER, at the end of the movie *Lost Horizon* (1937), from the novel by James Hilton

"Here's to a time when we were little girls and no one asked us to marry."
—JOAN CRAWFORD, *Humoresque*

"Here's to plain speaking and clear understanding."
—HUMPHREY BOGART, *The Maltese Falcon*

"Here's to those who wish us well, and those who don't can go to hell."
—JULIA LOUIS-DREYFUS as Elaine in *Seinfeld*

"I am, as ever, in bewildered awe of any couple who make the commitment that Angus and Laura have made this morning. True love is a very rare and splendid thing and I think we see it here today.

"This is only the second time I've ever been a best man. I hope I did the job all right that time. The couple in question at least are still talking to me. Unfortunately, they're not talking to each other. The divorce came through a couple of months ago."
—HUGH GRANT, *Four Weddings and a Funeral*

"I keep my friends close, but my enemies closer."
—MARLON BRANDO, *The Godfather*

"I would rather be with the people in this room, than with the finest people in the world."
—STEVE MARTIN as Cyrano in *Roxanne*

"Live long and prosper."
—LEONARD NIMOY, *Star Trek*

"May the force be with you."
—SIR ALEC GUINNESS, *Star Wars*

"My only rival, the United States cavalry."
—MAUREEN O'HARA as Mrs. Yorke in *Rio Grande* (1950), making a toast
at an officer's dinner party, having rejoined her husband, Colonel Kirby
Yorke (John Wayne) after fifteen years

"To long lives and short wars."
—HARRY MORGAN, as Colonel Sherman Potter in *M*A*S*H*

"To making it count."
—LEONARDO DICAPRIO, *Titanic*

"To peace and the American way of plumbing."
—ALAN ALDA as Hawkeye Pierce in *M*A*S*H*

"To the men we loved: the stinkers."
—EVE ARDEN, *Mildred Pierce*

CITIES AND TOWNS

There was a time when almost every city had at least one toast in its honor. A
sampling:

BOSTON
And this is good old Boston,
The home of the bean and the cod,
Where the Lowells talk to the Cabots,
And the Cabots talk only to God.
—DR. JOHN C. BOSSIDY, at a Holy Cross College alumni dinner

If you hear an owl hoot "to whom" instead of "to who," you can make
up your mind that he was born and educated in Boston.

Then here's to the City of Boston
The town of the cries and the groans
Where the Cabots can't see the Kobotschniks
And the Lowells won't speak to the Cohns.
—FRANKLIN P. ADAMS, in *So Much Velvet*

To self-satisfied Boston, always serene,
The land of the cultured, the home of the bean,
Where the erudite policemen, patrolling their beats,
Have nothing to watch but the crooks in the streets.

CHICAGO

Chicago sounds rough to the maker of verse;
One comfort we have—Cincinnati sounds worse.
—OLIVER WENDELL HOLMES

Here's to Chicago, where everything dates from the fair
Where they know the full value of good hot air
When there's prospect of business they'll always stand treat
For their hearts are as big as their women's feet.

Here's to dear old Chicago,
The home of the ham what 'am,
Where everyone speaks to his neighbor,
And nobody gives a damn.

Neither hog butcher nor broad-shouldered any longer, Chicago is a
lumbering hulk with a silly grin; too simple to play the gent, too open
to be phoney. That's why I'm so fond of it.
—STUDS TERKEL

To the horror of Dracula's fangs,
To the evil of Shakespeare's Iago;
Let the nightmares scare, they can't compare
To the snow and the cold of Chicago.
—BARRY BERENSON

HOLLYWOOD

Here's to Hollywood—
A place where people from Iowa
Mistake each other for movie stars.
—FRED ALLEN

NEW HAVEN

Here's to the town of New Haven,
The home of the truth and the light,
    Where God speaks to Jones,
    In the very same tones,
That he uses with Hadley and Dwight.
—DEAN JONES

NEW HAVEN AND BOSTON

Here's to New Haven and Boston,
And the turf that the Puritans trod
In the rest of mankind little virtue they find
But they feel quite chummy with God.
—WALTER FOSTER ANGELL

NEW YORK

Vulgar of manner, overfed,
Overdressed and underbred;
Crazed with avarice, lust and rum,
New York, thy name's Delirium.
—B. R. NEWTON, "Owed to New York," 1906

"OUR TOWN"

Here's to our town—a place where people spend money they haven't
earned to buy things they don't need to impress people they don't like.

Here's to the virgins of _____;
It's not very much we see of 'em.
Here's to those charming, beautiful girls;
Here's to them—all three of 'em.

PHILADELPHIA

All hail the tranquil village!
    May nothing jar its ease,
Where the spiders build their bridges
    From the trolleys to the trees.

On the whole I'd rather be in Philadelphia.
—W. C. FIELDS, composed when he was asked to write his own epitaph.
    It does not appear on his grave, as is often asserted.

To old Philadelphia, stately and slow;
As soon as you get there you're ready to go.
That peaceful city of the dead,
Where the greatest excitement is going to bed.

PITTSBURGH

Here's to Pittsburgh; and may it suit you
As it has sooted me!

SAN FRANCISCO

Here's to old 'Frisco, out on the coast
The American Paris, her favorite boast
Once in every nine minutes
Just watch them and time it
They'll sing you that song of the glorious climate.

WASHINGTON

First in war, first in peace, and last in the American League.
—This allusion to the long-suffering Washington Senators baseball team has
    new relevance in the twenty-first century, although the new team is in the
    National League and, as of this writing, in the summer of 2009, deeply
    mired in last place in the NL East.

COLLEGES AND UNIVERSITIES

GEORGIA

Here's to the lass who serves the drinks,
And to the man who picks up the check.
And here's to the Georgia bulldogs and
To hell with Georgia Tech.
—LEWIS GRIZZARD, from *A Gentleman's Guide to Toasting*

GEORGIA TECH

I'd drink to ev'ry fellow who comes far and near;
I'm a rambling wreck from Georgia Tech and a hell of an engineer!

HARVARD

As I was going to Harvard Square,
I met a man who didn't care.
He didn't care again today.
How long has Harvard been that way?

Cambridge is a famous town,
Both for wit and knowledge,
Some they whip and some they hang,
And some they send to college.
—From a time of stocks and pillories

Here's to Johnny Harvard;
Fill him up a full glass,
Fill him up a glass to his name and fame,
And at the same time
Don't forget his true love;
Fill her up a bumper to the brim.

M.I.T.

E to the U, DU-DX;
E to the X;
DX;
Cosine, secant, tangent, sine,
3.14159;
Integral, radical, U DV;
Slipstick, slide rule, M.I.T.

—Cheer, repeated in the *Sporting News* of October 1988, on returning to
  college football after an eighty-seven-year absence

Of course I like the M.I.T.,
Jolly place for fun, you see,
You can work from nine to six by day,
And from seven to one, at night, they say,
And go to bed with an aching head
And a weary sense of work undone,
And a wonder strong as to where's the fun
If you study at M.I.T.

NORTHWESTERN

That's all right,
That's OK,
You're gonna work
For us someday.

—Cheer to victors over the school's long-suffering football team

PRINCETON

I wish I had a barrel of rum
And sugar three hundred pounds,
With the chapel bell to put in it
And the clapper to sit it 'round,
I'd drink to the health of Nassau boys,
And the girls both far and near,
For I'm a rambling rank of poverty,
And a son of a gambolier.

VASSAR

And so you see, for old V.C.
Our love shall never fail.
Full well we know
That all we owe
To Matthew Vassar's ale!

—Vassar song refering to the Poughkeepsie ale brewer who founded the
college

YALE

For God, for Country, and for Yale.

For we think it is but right, sir,
On Wednesday and Saturday night, sir,
To get most gloriously tight, sir,
    To drive dull care away.
It is a way we have at old Yale, sir,
    To drive dull care away.

Let him be kept from paper, pen, and ink.
That he may cease to write and learn to think.

SEE ALSO: *Reunions; Special Occasions (Graduation)*

CURSES

A toast in reverse is a curse—the flip side of a blessing. In form, they are alike,
right down to the common openings of "Here's to" and "May you." Here, in
English, is a sampling largely drawn from the two great sources of maledic-
tion, Gaelic and Yiddish. Use these with caution—according to an old super-
stition, curses, like chickens, tend to come home to roost.

A plague on both your houses.
—WILLIAM SHAKESPEARE, *Romeo and Juliet*, Act III

But blast the man, with curses loud and deep,
Whate'er the rascal's name, or age, or station,
Who first invented, and went round advising,
That artificial cut-off, Early Rising!
—John Godfrey Saxe, "Early Rising"

Corns should grow on your nose.
—Yiddish

Here's to short shoes and long corns to our enemies.
—Irish

Lord, confound this surly sister,
Blight her brow with blotch and blister,
Cramp her larynx, lung, and liver,
In her guts a galling give her.

Let her live to earn her dinners
In Mountjoy with seedy sinners:
Lord, this judgement quickly bring,
And I'm Your servant, J. M. Synge.
—John Millington Synge, Irish dramatist and author of "The
    Playboy of the Western World," who wrote "The Curse" to a sister of an
    enemy who disapproved of his writing

May a band of gypsies camp in your belly and train bears to dance on
your liver.
—Yiddish

May all your enemies move in with you.
—Yiddish

May each of your days be worse than the last and may you live forever.
—Irish

May every old fairy from Cork to Dunleary,
Dip him snug and airy in river or lake,

68

Where the eel and the trout may dine on the snout,
Of the monster that murdered Nell Flaherty's drake.
—Verse from the Irish cursing song "Nell Flaherty's Drake"

May his cradle ne'er rock, may his box have no lock,
May his wife have no frock for to cover her back,
May his cock never crow, may his bellows ne'er blow,
And his pipe and his pot, may he ever more lack.
—Irish, a curse to an informer

May his pig never grunt, may his cat never hunt,
That a ghost may catch him in the dark of the night,
May his hen never lay, may his ass never bray,
And his goat fly away like an old paper kite.
—Irish

May his soul be forever tormented by fire and his bones be dug up by
dogs and dragged through the streets of Minneapolis.
—GARRISON KEILLOR, in *Happy to Be Here*

May his spade never dig.
May his sow never pig.
May each hair in his wig be well thrashed with a flail.
May his door never latch.
May his turkeys not hatch.
May the rats eat his mail.

May she marry a ghost, and bear him a kitten, and may the high king
of glory permit it to get the mange.
—Irish

May the devil cut the toes off all our foes, that we may know them by
their limping.
—Irish

May the devil make a ladder of your backbone while he is picking apples in the garden of hell.
—Irish

May the greatest doctors in the world know of your case.
—Yiddish

May the seven seas not be enough for your enemas.
—Yiddish

May you be alone in paradise.
—Yiddish

May you be proof that a human being can endure anything.
—Yiddish

May you grow so rotten that goats, skunks, and pigs refuse to be near you.
—Yiddish

May you never develop stomach trouble from too rich a diet.
—Yiddish

May you never go to hell, but always be on your way.
—Yiddish

May you turn into a sparrow and owe your existence to the droppings of a horse.
—Yiddish

May your buttocks fall off.
—Yiddish

May your finger get stuck in your nose.
—Irish

May your nose run and your feet smell.
—Yiddish

May your retirement plan be supervised by Jimmy Hoffa.*
—STEVE ALLEN

May your sex life be as good as your credit.
—Yiddish

Pieces should fall off you.
—Yiddish

That all your teeth should fall out—but one should remain for a toothache.
—Yiddish

To the enemies of our country! May they have cobweb breeches, a porcupine saddle, a hard-trotting horse and an eternal journey.
—Popular American Revolution–era toast, which took the form of a curse

You should grow like an onion with your feet in the air and your head in the ground.
—Yiddish

You should have a child through the ribs.
—Yiddish

SEE ALSO: *Hell and Damnation*

---

* Hoffa was the head of the Teamsters who spent fifteen years in jail for corruption. A modern version of the curse might end with Bernard Madoff.

DEATH

Ah, make we the most of what we may yet spend,
Before we too into the Dust descend;
Dust into Dust, and under Dust to lie,
Sans wine, sans song, sans singer, and sans end.
—OMAR KHAYYÁM

All care to the wind we merrily fling,
For the damp, cold grave is a dead sure thing!
It's a dead sure thing we're alive tonight
And the damp, cold grave is out of sight.
—ERNEST JARROLD, toast of the Vampire Club

Cause of Death: Life.
—TOM BOSWELL, epitaph for Bill Veeck in the *Washington Post*, May 31, 1981

Here's to death, because death will give me one last bier.

Here's to those who have gone ahead to the great tavern where we
shall all meet again.
—CEDRIC DICKENS, grandson of Charles Dickens and steward of his
   legacy, who gave the toast at the Dickens events he staged

Life is a jest; and all things show it.
I thought so once; but now I know it.
—JOHN GAY, epitaph on his tomb in Westminster Abbey

May every hair on your head turn into a candle to light your way to
heaven, and may God and His Holy Mother take the harm of the
years away from you.
—Irish

May we all come to peaceful ends,
And leave our debts unto our friends.

Oh, here's to other meetings,
 And merry greetings then;
And here's to those we've drunk with,
 But never can again.

Over their hallowed graves may the winds of heaven whisper hourly
benedictions.

She drank good ale, good punch and wine
And lived to the age of 99.
—Epitaph for Rebecca Freeland at Edwalton, Nottinghamshire, 1741

Take lightly that which heavy lies;
what all respect, do you despair;
some flippancy your soul may save.
—A goose is walking on your grave.
—PEGGY BACON, "Motto," quoted in "Peggy Bacon's World,"
 the *Boston Globe*, July 8, 1979

Though life is now pleasant and sweet to the sense
We'll be damnably moldy a hundred years hence.
—Old pirate toast

Time cuts down all,
Both great and small.

'Tis my will when I die, not a tear shall be shed,
No *Hic Jacet* be graved on my stone,
But pour o'er my coffin a bottle of red,
And write that *His Drinking Is Done*.

To Death, the jolly old bouncer, now
Our glasses let's be clinking;
If he hadn't put other out, I trow,
To-night we'd not be drinking.
—OLIVER HERFORD

To live in hearts we leave behind is not to die.

Wash me when dead in the juice of the vine, dear friends!
Let your funeral service be drinking and wine, dear friends!
And if you would meet again when the Doomsday comes,
Search the dust of the tavern, and sift from it mine, dear friends!
We toast his roguish and venerable shade.
—JAMES J. KILPATRICK, toast to H. L. Mencken on the 101st anniversary
    of Mencken's birth, quoted in the *Baltimore Sun*, September 13, 1981

ENGLAND

Daddy Neptune, one day, to Freedom did say,
If ever I lived upon dry land,
The spot I would hit on would be little Britain!
Says Freedom, "Why that's my own island!"
O, it's a snug little island!
A right little, tight little island!
Search the world round, none can be found
So happy as this little island.

England! my country, great and free!
Heart of the world, I drink to thee!

First pledge our Queen this solemn night,
    Then drink to England, every guest;
That man's the best Cosmopolite
    Who loves his native country best.
—ALFRED, LORD TENNYSON, "Hands All Round"

In English beer,
With an English cheer,
To the right little,
Tight little island!

Let us sing our own treasures, Old England's good cheer,
To the profits and pleasures of stout British beer;
Your wine-tippling, dram-sipping fellows retreat,
But your beer-drinking Britons can never be beat.
The French with their vineyards and meager pale ale,
They drink from the squeezing of half-ripe fruit;
But we, who have hop-yards to mellow our ale,
Are rosy and plump and have freedom to boot.
—English drinking song, circa 1757

O England!—model to thy inward greatness,
Like little body with a mighty heart.
—WILLIAM SHAKESPEARE, *Henry V*, Act II

Our friends are coming, our friends are coming.
—GEORGE H. W. BUSH, from the vice president's toast at the
    British embassy during the visit of the Prince and Princess of Wales,
    November 11, 1985

St. George he was for England,
And before he killed the dragon
He drank a pint of English ale
Out of an English flagon.
—G. K. CHESTERTON

EXCUSES FOR THE GLASS

In Richard Brinsley Sheridan's comedy *The School for Scandal*, Sir Harry
Bumper recites the quintessential example of a toast that is more an "excuse
for the glass" than an expression of anything else.

Starting with the full version of Sheridan's toast, here is a collection of
excuses dedicated to such concerns as fleas and riotous monks.

Here's to the maiden of bashful fifteen;
    Here's to the widow of fifty;
Here's to the flaunting extravagant queen,
    And here's to the housewife that's thrifty.
        Let the toast pass—
        Drink to the lass—
I'll warrant she'll prove an excuse for the glass.

Here's to the charmer whose dimples we prize;
    Now to the maid who has none, sir;
Here's to the girl with a pair of blue eyes,
    And here's to the nymph with but one, sir.
        Let the toast pass—
        Drink to the lass—
I'll warrant she'll prove an excuse for the glass.

Here's to the maid with a bosom of snow;
    Now to her that's as brown as a berry;
Here's to the wife with a face full of woe,
    And now for the damsel that's merry.
        Let the toast pass—
        Drink to the lass—
I'll warrant she'll prove an excuse for the glass.

For let 'em be clumsy, or let 'em be slim,
    Young or ancient, I care not a feather;
So fill a pint bumper quite up to the brim,
    And let us e'en toast 'em together.
        Let the toast pass—
        Drink to the lass—
I'll warrant she'll prove an excuse for the glass.
—RICHARD BRINSLEY SHERIDAN, *The School for Scandal*, Act III

Great fleas have lesser fleas,
    And these have less to bite 'em;
These fleas have lesser fleas,
    And so ad infinitum.

The great fleas themselves in turn,
    Have greater fleas to go on.
While these again have greater still,
    And greater still, and so on.

Here's to the bee—the busy soul;
He has no time for birth control.
That's why it is, in times like these,
We have so many sons of bees!

Here's to the happy, bounding flea:
You cannot tell the he from the she,
But he can tell, and so can she!
—ROLAND YOUNG

I used to know a clever toast,
    But pshaw! I cannot think it—
So fill your glass to anything
    And, bless your souls, I'll drink it.

May riotous monks have a double Lent.

May the skin of your bum never cover a drum.

May we never put our finger in another man's pie.

She's pretty to walk with:
And witty to talk with;
And pleasant too to think on.
But the best use of all
Is, her health is a stale,
And helps us to make us drink on.
—SIR JOHN SUCKLING

There's many a toast I'd like to say,
If I could only think it;
So fill your glass to anything,
And thank the Lord, I'll drink it!
—WALLACE IRWIN

SEE ALSO: *Bulls; Limericks; Tongue Twisters; World's Worst Toasts*

EXPECTANT PARENTS

Here is the toast of the moon and the stars,
To the child . . . who will soon be ours.

Here's to one who born will be,
Born of the body, sowed of the soul,
Born of the flesh of you and me.

Out of a love our child will grow . . .
Greater than light, deeper than dark,
All other love is but a spark.

FISHING

For some unexplained reason, a relatively large number of fishing toasts exist while there are few for other sports and pastimes. (Incidentally, fishing also inspired one of the great provincial headlines of all time, which appeared in a Lenox, Massachusetts, newspaper on January 6, 1933: PRESIDENT COOLIDGE DEAD—MAY HAVE FISHED HERE.)

A bad day of fishing is still better than a good day at work.
—Bumper sticker

A fisherman, 'twixt you and I
Will very seldom tell a lie—
Except when it is needed to
Describe the fish that left his view.

Behold the fisherman!
He riseth in the early morning
And disturbeth the whole
    household.

Enjoy thy stream, O harmless fish,
And when an angler for his dish,
    Through gluttony's vile sin,
Attempts, the wretch, to pull thee out,
God give thee strength, O gentle trout,
    To pull the rascal in.

Fishing is the chance to wash one's soul with pure air. It brings
meekness and inspiration, reduces our egotism, soothes our troubles
and shames our wickedness.
—HERBERT HOOVER, quoted in the *New York Herald Tribune*,
    May 19, 1947

Health to men,
And death to fish;
They're wagging the tails
That will pay for this.

Here's to fishing—a grand delusion enthusiastically promoted by
glorious liars in old clothes.
—DON MARQUIS

Here's to our fisherman bold,
Here's to the fish he caught;
Here's to the one that got away,
And here's to the one he bought.

Here's to the fish that I may catch;
So large that even I,
When talking of it afterward,
Will never need to lie.

May the holes in your net be no bigger than your fish.
—Irish

On an Assyrian tablet of 2000 B.C. we find the following: "The gods do not subtract from the allotted span of men's lives the hours spent in fishing."
—HERBERT HOOVER

Rod and line: May they never part company.

Simon Peter saith unto them, I go afishing; they say unto him, we also go with thee.
—John 21:3

The joy of fishing—is fishing.
—HARLAN H. BALLARD

The steady fisherman—who never "reels home."

There are more fish taken out of a stream than ever were in it.
—OLIVER HERFORD

To the fish—a creature that goes on vacation at about the same time most fishermen do.

A full belly, a heavy purse, and a light heart.

According to the Spanish proverb, four persons are wanted to make a good salad; a spendthrift for oil, a miser for vinegar, a counsellor for salt, and a madman to stir all up.
—Abraham Hayward, *The Art of Dining*

All human history attests
That happiness to man—the
    hungry sinner—
Since Eve ate apples, much depends on dinner!
—Lord Byron

Better is a dinner of herbs where love is, than a fatted ox and hatred.
—Ancient proverb

Eat, drink, and be merry, for tomorrow you diet.

Eat well's drink well's brother.
—Old Scottish proverb

Good pies and strong beer.
—*Poor Robin's Almanack*, 1695

Health to our bodies, peace to our minds, and plenty to our boards.
—Eighteenth-century pre-dinner toast

"I was always religiously inclined," said the oyster as he slid down the minister's throat. "But ne'er did I dream I'd enter the clergy."

I'd rather have a dinner while I'm living than a monument when I'm dead, for the dinner will be on my friends, while the monument would be on me.

Let the dogs wait a long time.
—Irish wish for a lengthy and ample dinner

May they have sugar to their strawberries!
—LEIGH HUNT, translated from an unidentified Italian poet, 1840

May you always have red-eye gravy with your ham, hush puppies with your catfish, and the good sense not to argue with your wife.
—Toast from Tennessee, quoted by Timothy Noah in the *New Republic*

O hour of all hours, the most blessed upon earth, the blessed hour of our dinners!
—EDWARD GEORGE LYTTON

On the table spread the cloth,
    Let the knives be sharp and clean;
Pickles get and salad both,
    Let them each be fresh and green.

Only the truly mad eat alone, like Howard Hughes and Stalin.
—GUY DAVENPORT

Serenely full, the epicure would say,
Fate cannot harm me, I have dined today.

To eat, to drink, and to be merry.
—Ecclesiastes 8:15

To Gasteria, the tenth Muse, who presides over the enjoyments of Taste.
—ANTHELME BRILLAT-SAVARIN

To Mom's cooking: May my wife never find out how bad it really was.

To soup: May it be seen and not heard.

Unquiet meals make ill digestions.
—WILLIAM SHAKESPEARE, *The Comedy of Errors*, Act V

We may live without poetry, music and art;
We may live without conscience, and live without heart;
We may live without friends; we may live without books;
But civilized man cannot live without cooks.
We may live without books—what is knowledge but grieving?
We may live without hope—what is hope but deceiving?
We may live without love—what is passion but pining?
But where is the man that can live without dining?
—Owen Meredith, "Lucile"

Who can believe with common sense,
A bacon slice gives God offence?
Or how a herring hath a charm
Almighty vengeance to disarm?
Wrapt up in majesty divine,
Does he regard on what we dine?
—Jonathan Swift

With small beer, good ale and wine,
O ye gods! how I shall dine!

SEE ALSO: *Cheeses; Graces; Professional and Occupational (Cooking)*

FRIENDSHIP

A day for toil, an hour for sport,
But for a friend life is too short.
—Ralph Waldo Emerson

A health to you,
A wealth to you,
And the best that life, can give to you.
May fortune still be kind to you.
And happiness be true to you,
And life be long and good to you,
Is the toast of all your friends to you.

Absent friends—though out of sight we recognize them with our glasses.

Don't walk in front of me,
    I may not follow.
Don't walk behind me,
    I may not lead.
Walk beside me,
    And just be my friend.
—Irish

Friendship: May differences of opinion cement it.

Friendship's the wine of life.
Let's drink of it and to it.

Here's all that's fine to you!
Books and old wine to you!
Girls be divine to you!
—Richard Hovey

Here's to a friend. He knows you well and likes you just the same.

Here's to beefsteak when you're hungry,
Whiskey when you are dry,
Greenbacks when you are busted,
And Heaven when you die!

Here's to cold nights, warm friends, and a good drink to give them.

Here's to eternity—may we spend it in as good company as this night finds us.

Here's to our friends . . . and the strength to put up with them.
—Line used in ads for the movie *The Four Seasons*

Here's to our friendship;
May it be reckoned long as a lifetime,
Close as a second.

Here's to you, old friend, may you live a thousand years,
Just to sort of cheer things in this vale of human tears;
And may I live a thousand too—a thousand—less a day,
'Cause I wouldn't care to be on Earth and hear you'd passed away.

I drink to the brew of our friendship; it goes to my heart, but never to my head.
—Anonymous

It is around the table that friends understand best the warmth of being together.
—Old Italian saying

I've traveled many a highway
I've walked for many a mile
Here's to the people who made my day
To the people who waved and smiled.
—Tom T. Hall, from *A Gentleman's Guide to Toasting*

May the friends of our youth be the companions of our old age.

May the hinges of friendship never rust, nor the wings of love lose a feather.
—Dean Ramsay, in *Reminiscences of Scottish Life*

May we have more and more friends, and need them less and less.

May we never have friends who, like shadows, follow us in sunshine only to desert us on a cloudy day.

May your tobacco never run out, your library never turn musty, your cellar never go dry, and your friends never turn foes.

My boat is on the shore,
    And my bark is on the sea;
But, before I go, Tom Moore,
    Here's a double health to thee.
—Lord Byron, to Thomas Moore

Never drink anything without first smelling it,
Never sign anything without first reading it.
Never dive into pools of depth unknown,
And rarely drink—if you are alone.
—Seventeenth-century philosophy

Now I, friend, drink to you, friend,
    As my friend drank to me,
And I, friend, charge you, friend,
    As my friend charged me,
That you, friend, drink to your friend,
    As my friend drank to me;
And the more we drink together, friend,
    The merrier we'll be!

Old friends are scarce,
New friends are few;
Here's hoping I've found
One of each in you.

Pour deep the rosy wine and drink a toast with me;
Here's to three: Thee, Wine, and Camaraderie!
—THOMAS MOORE

The Lord gives us our relatives,
Thank God we can choose our friends.

The world is gay and colorful,
And life itself is new.
And I am very grateful for
The friend I found in you.

Then here's to thee, old friend; and long
        May thou and I thus meet,
To brighten still with wine and song
        This short life ere it fleet.

To friends: as long as we are able
To lift our glasses from the table.

To my friend: If we ever disagree, may you be in the right.

To our best friends, who know the worst about us but refuse to
believe it.

To the spirit of Christmases yet to come.
—World War II toast

We'll drink the wanting into wealth,
And those that languish into health,
The afflicted into joy,
the oppressed into serenity and rest.
—CHARLES COTTON

We'll think of all the friends we know
And drink to all worth drinking to.

Were't the last drop in the well,
        As I gasp'd upon the brink,
Ere my fainting spirit fell,
        'Tis to thee I would drink.

SEE ALSO: *Alliterative; Biblical; General; Guests; Hosts and Hostesses; Love; Old Things; Parting*

GENERAL

A handsome new nose to you.

A little health, a little wealth,
        A little house and freedom:
With some few friends for certain ends
        But little cause to need 'em.

A toast to the wise
        And a toast to the foolish
A toast to your eyes—
        May they never grow mulish!

Ad multos annos—to many years!
—MARIO CUOMO, governor of New York, to President Ronald Reagan at
    the 1988 Gridiron Club dinner, Washington, D.C.

All that gives you pleasure.

All true hearts and sound bottoms.

And fill them high with generous juice,
As generous as your mind,
And pledge me in the generous toast—
The whole of human kind!
—ROBERT BURNS

Be glad of life!
Because it gives you the chance to love and work,
To play and to look up at the stars.
—HENRY VAN DYKE

Be not concerned if thou findest thyself in possession of unexpected
wealth. Allah will provide an unexpected use for it.
—JAMES JEFFREY ROCHE

Blue skies and green lights.

Call frequently,
Drink moderately,
Part friendly,
Pay today,
Trust tomorrow.

Days of Ease and Nights of Pleasure.

Delicious nights to every virtuous heart.

'Ere's to the 'ealth o' your Royal 'ighness; 'and may the skin o' ha
gooseberry be big enough for han humbrella to cover hup hall your
henemies.
—CADDY'S toast in *Erminie*

Good company, good wine, good welcome can make good people.
—WILLIAM SHAKESPEARE, *Henry VIII*, Act I

Good day, good health, good cheer, good night!

Health to my body, wealth to my purse,
Heaven to my soul, and I wish you no worse.

Heaven give thee many, many merry days!
—WILLIAM SHAKESPEARE, *Merry Wives of Windsor*, Act V

Here's a toast to all who are here,
No matter where you're from;
May the best day you have seen
Be worse than your worst to come.

Here's hoping how and hoping who
      And hoping when and where;
And may all good things come to you
      Before you cease to care.

Here's to all of us.
—Sir Thomas Lipton

Here's to beauty, wit, and wine, and to a full stomach, a full purse,
and a light heart.

Here's to us that are here, to you that are there, and the rest of us
everywhere.
—Rudyard Kipling

Here's to your good health, and your family's good health, and may
you all live long and prosper.
—Joseph Jefferson as Rip Van Winkle

Here's tow'ds yer an' tew yer!
'F I never had met yet
I'd never hev knewed yer.

I drink to the days that are.
—William Morris

I wish thee health,
I wish thee wealth,
I wish thee gold in store,
I wish thee heaven upon earth—
What could I wish thee more?

If you have an appetite for life, stay hungry.

In the garden of life, may your pea pods never be empty.
—BILL COPELAND in the Sarasota *Journal*, quoted in *Reader's Digest*,
    June 1982

It is best to rise from life as from the banquet, neither thirsty nor
drunken.
—ARISTOTLE

Love to one, friendship to many, and good will to all.

Make every day a masterpiece.

Make the most of life while you may,
Life is short and wears away!
—WILLIAM OLDYS

May life last as long as it is worth wearing.

May our faults be written on the seashore, and every good action
prove a wave to wash them out.

May our feast days be many and our fast days be few.
—MARY L. BOOTH

May the clouds in your life form only a background for a lovely sunset.

May the most you wish for be the least you get.

May those who deceive us be always deceived.

May we all live in pleasure and die out of debt.

May we be happy and our enemies know it. May we live respected and
die regretted.

May we breakfast with Health, dine with Friendship, crack a bottle with Mirth, and sup with the goddess Contentment.

May we live to learn well, and learn to live well.

May we never do worse.

May we never feel want, nor ever want feeling.

May we never flatter our superiors or insult our inferiors.

May we never know want till relief is at hand.

May you always distinguish between the weeds and the flowers.

May you be merry and lack nothing.
—William Shakespeare

May you get it all together before you come apart.
—Bill Leary, quoted in *Reader's Digest*, June 1982

May you have the hindsight to know where you've been . . . the foresight to know where you're going.
—Charles M. Meyers

May you have warmth in your igloo, oil in your lamp, and peace in your heart.
—Eskimo toast

May you live all the days of your life.
—Jonathan Swift

May you live as long as you want to and want to as long as you live.

May your life be as beautiful as a summer day with just enough clouds to make you appreciate the sunshine.
—Found inscribed in a book and dated 1882

So live that when you come to die, even the undertaker will feel sorry
for you.
—MARK TWAIN

Success to the lover, honor to the brave,
Health to the sick, and freedom to the slave.

The riotous enjoyment of a quiet conscience.

The three generals in power: General Employment, General Industry,
and General Comfort.

There is no satiety
In our society
With the variety
of your *esprit*.
Here's a long purse to you,
And a great thirst to you!
Fate be no worse to you
Than she's been to me!

'Tis hard to tell which is best,
music, food, drink, or rest.

'Tis not so bad a world,
As some would like to make it;
But whether good or whether bad,
Depends on how you take it.

To the old, long life and treasure;
To the young, all health and pleasure;
    To the fair, their face,
    With eternal grace;
And the rest, to be loved at leisure.
—BEN JONSON

Two ins and one out—in health, in wealth, and out of debt.

While we live, let us live.

Wit without virulence, wine without excess, and wisdom without affectation.

You shall and you shan't,
     You will and you won't,
You're condemned if you do,
And you are damned if you don't.

GRACES

Be present at our table, Lord.
Be here and everywhere adored.
These mercies bless, and grant that we
May feast in Paradise with Thee.
—JOHN CENNICK, 1741

Bless, O Lord, these delectable vittles;
May they add to your glory,
not to our middles.
—Twentieth-century American grace

Bless, O Lord, this food to our use, and us to Thy service,
and make us ever needful of the needs of others, in Jesus' name, Amen.
—Traditional Protestant grace

Bless these thy gifts, most gracious God,
From whom all goodness springs;
Make clean our hearts and feed our souls
With good and joyful things.

Bless this food and us that eats it.
—Cowboy grace

Bless us, O Lord, and these Thy gifts which we have received
out of Thy bounty, through Christ Our Lord. Amen.
—Traditional Catholic grace

Come, Lord Jesus, be our guest, and let Thy gifts to us be blessed.
Amen.

For a' Thou'st placed upon the table, we thank the Lord, as well's
we're able.

For health and strength and daily food,
We praise thy name, O Lord.

For rabbits young and rabbits old,
For rabbits hot, and rabbits cold,
For rabbits tender, rabbits tough,
We thank Thee, Lord, we've had enough!
—JONATHAN SWIFT, who undoubtedly suffered from an endless round
    of luncheons in his honor, just as today's celebrities do. But whereas
    the modern complaint might be of too much chicken, Swift's lament
    was different.

For the air we breathe,
and the water we drink,
For a soul and a mind
with which to think,
For food that comes
from fertile sod,
For these, and many things
I'm thankful to my God.
—Thanksgiving grace written by comedian Danny Thomas when he was in
    sixth grade

For Thy benefits, O Lord, we give Thee thanks.
—Grace after meat

For what we are about to receive, the Lord make us truly thankful, for
Christ's sake. Amen.
—Old English classic, which is probably the best known of all Christian
    English-language graces

Give me a good digestion, Lord,
    And also something to digest;
Give me a healthy body, Lord,
    And sense to keep it at its best.
—Dr. Furse, bishop of St. Albans

God bless the master of this house,
God bless the mistress too;
And all the little children
Who round the table go.
—Traditional British grace

God is great, God is good,
We will thank Him for this food.
By His hand must all be fed
Thanks be to God for our daily bread.
—Traditional children's grace

Good bread, good meat
Good God, let's eat!

Heavenly father bless us,
And keep us all alive;
There's ten of us for dinner
And not enough for five.

Here a little child I stand
Heaving up my either hand;
Cold as paddocks though they be,
Here I lift them up to Thee,
For a benison to fall
On our meat, and on us all.
Amen.
—Robert Herrick, "Another Grace for a Child"

Lift up your hands toward the sanctuary and bless the Lord. Blessed art Thou, O Lord our God, King of the Universe, who brings forth bread from the earth. Amen.
—Traditional Jewish thanksgiving before meals

Lord God, we thank you for all the good things you provide, and we pray for the time when people everywhere shall have the abundance they need.

MA KETTLE: "Say grace, Pa."
PA KETTLE (removing his hat, looking up): "Much obliged, Lord."
—Scene from a Ma and Pa Kettle movie in which they are seated at a
  bountiful table surrounded by her large family

May the good Lord take a liking to you—but not too soon!

May the holy Saints be about your bed, and about your board, from this time to the latter end—God help us all!
—Irish

May the Lord make us thankful for what we are about to receive, and for what Mr. Jones hath already received. Amen.
—Grace used to rebuke anyone who starts eating too soon

May the peace and blessing of God
descend upon us as we receive of his bounty,
and may our hearts be filled
with love for one another.

O Lord above, send us thy grace
     to be our stay,
So as we never do that which brings
     unto the wicked sinful way,
The wicked sinful way.
—THOMAS WHYTHORNE. This grace was sung and is believed to be one
  used by the Pilgrims on the *Mayflower*.

O Lord, we thank you for the gifts of your bounty,
which we enjoy at this table.
As you have provided for us in the past,
so may you sustain us throughout our lives.
While we enjoy your gifts,
may we never forget the needy and those in want.

O thou that blest the loaves and fishes,
Look down upon these two poor dishes,
And tho' the murphies* are but small,
O make them large enough for all,
For if they do our bellies fill
I'm sure it is a miracle.

Praise to God who giveth meat,
Convenient unto all to eat;
Praise for tea and buttered toast
Father, Son, and Holy Ghost.
—Old Scottish grace

Pray for peace and grace and spiritual food,
For wisdom and guidance, for all these are good,
But don't forget the potatoes.
—J. T. PETTEE, "Prayer and Potatoes"

"Pray God bless us all," said jolly Robin,
"And our meat within this place;
A cup of sack good, to nourish our blood,
And so I do end my grace."
—From "Robin Hood and the Butcher," *Oxford Book of Ballads*

---

* Murphies are potatoes.

Some have meat but cannot eat;
Some could eat but have no meat;
We have meat and can all eat;
Blest, therefore, be God for our meat.
—The Selkirk Grace, found in the papers of Dr. Plume of Maldon, Essex, in
    a handwriting of about 1650

Some hae meat, and canna eat,
    And some wad eat that want it
But we hae meat, and we can eat,
    And sae the Lord be thankit.
—Attributed to Robert Burns, and the version invoked at traditional Burns
    Night celebrations*

Thank the Lord for what we've gotten,
If ther 'ad been mooar, mooar we shud hev etten.

To God who gives us daily bread
A thankful song we raise,
And pray that he who sends us food
Will fill our hearts with praise.

We thank thee, Father, for thy care
And for thy bounty everywhere;
For this and every other gift,
Our grateful hearts to thee we lift.

What we are about to receive, may the Trinity and Unity bless, Amen.
—Grace before meat

---

* The birthday of Robert Burns, the well-known Scottish poet, was January 25,
and it has become traditional to gather for a meal on or near this date—with
haggis as the main dish. The first Burns Night celebration took place shortly after
his death in 1796. Various toasts, usually made with whiskey, are proposed
during or after the meal, which is usually followed by a program of songs, poems,
and dances. Traditionally, the supper begins with a recitation of the Selkirk
Grace and a bowl of broth, followed by the dramatic arrival of the haggis.

GUESTS

Here's to our guest—
Don't let him rest.
But keep his elbow bending.
'Tis time to drink—
Full time to think
Tomorrow—when you're mending.

May our house always be too small to hold all our friends.
—MYRTLE REED

Our house is ever at your service.

See, your guests approach:
Address yourself to entertain them sprightly,
And let's be red with mirth.
—WILLIAM SHAKESPEARE, *The Winter's Tale*, Act IV

Stay happy, my friend, hang easy and loose
Gettin' rattlesnake-riled is just no use
So here is a slogan that's sure hard to match
There ain't no use itchin' unless you can scratch!
—Cowboy welcome from a sampler

The ornament of a house is the guests who frequent it.

To our guest! A friend of our friend's is doubly our friend. Here's to him.

You are welcome here
Be at your ease
Get up when ready
Go to bed when you please.
Happy to share with you
Such as we've got
The leaks in the roof

The soup in the pot.
You don't have to thank us
Or laugh at our jokes
Sit deep and come often
You're one of the folks.
—Notice found in an Aspen, Colorado, guesthouse and quoted by Erica
   Wilson in the *Washington Post*, 1980

SEE ALSO: *Friendship; General; Hosts and Hostesses; Parting*

HALLOWEEN

From ghoulies and ghosties
And long-leggedy beasties
And things that go bump in the night,
Good Lord, deliver us!
—Prayer from Cornwall known as the "Cornish Litany." It was first printed in
   Frederick Thomas Nettleinghame's *Polperro Proverbs and Others*, published
   in 1926 by the Cornish Arts Association, but it's certainly much older.

Now it is the time of night
That the graves, all gaping wide,
Every one lets forth his sprite,
In the church-way paths to glide.
—WILLIAM SHAKESPEARE, *A Midsummer Night's Dream*, Act V. The line,
   uttered by Puck, is not specifically referring to Halloween, but the
   sentiment conjures up images of the day.

The evening of October thirty-one is Hallowe'en or Nut Crack Night.
It is clearly a relic of pagan times but it is still very popular. It is a
night set apart for walking about and playing harmless pranks, such
as placing the hotel omnibus on top of the Baptist church or plugging
the milkman's pump.
—KIN HUBBARD

When black cats prowl and pumpkins gleam,
May luck be yours on Halloween.
—Postcard greeting, circa 1920

SEE ALSO: *Curses, Hell and Damnation*

HEALTH

Early to rise and early to bed
makes a male healthy and wealthy and dead.
—JAMES THURBER

Here's a health to every one;
Peace on earth, and heaven won.

Here's to your health—a long life and an easy death to you.

Here's to your health! You make age curious, time furious, and all of us envious.

That a doctor might never earn a dollar out of you—and that your heart may never give out.

The best doctors in the world are Doctor Diet, Doctor Quiet, and Doctor Merryman.
—JONATHAN SWIFT

The health of the salmon to you: a long life, a full heart, and a wet mouth!
—Irish

To your good health, old friend,
may you live for a thousand years,
and I be there to count them.
—ROBERT SMITH SURTEES

SEE ALSO: *Alliterative; Friendship; General*

HELL AND DAMNATION

Here's to Hell!
May the stay there
Be as much fun as the way there!

Here's to Mephisto! Goodness knows
What we would do without him.
And, good Mephisto, do not spurn
Our toast with mocking laughter;
Nor yet the compliment return
But toasting us hereafter.
—OLIVER HERFORD

Here's to the pavement of Hell,
And the tiresome old teachers who talk it.
Observation has taught
That we shall not be caught
Entirely alone, when we walk it.

Here's to you
Here's to me
May we never disagree.
But, if we do,
to Hell with you—
and here's to me!

Up friends, up!
    Tonight we sup,
Though tomorrow we die of revel!
    Rise for a toast,
    Though tomorrow we roast;
To hell to His Lordship, the Devil!

SEE ALSO: *Curses, Halloween*

HINTS FOR EFFECTIVE TOASTING WITH LESSONS FROM HISTORY

1. *Do it in a way that is most comfortable to you.* You may remain seated. Legend has it that it became acceptable to toast without standing in Britain during the reign of Charles II. The king allowed that this would be acceptable after he had risen in response to a toast in his honor while aboard the ship *Royal Charles* and bashed his head into a beam. A similar bashing to King William IV, when he was heir to the throne and toasted George IV while aboard a man-of-war, forever ended the custom of standing toasts in the Royal Navy.

2. *Don't mix toasts with other messages.* During World War II, at a banquet given by Joseph Stalin at the Russian embassy in Tehran, Stalin rose to his feet after Churchill, Roosevelt, and other leaders had been toasted. He grinned and made a quick, impromptu remark in Russian. Judging from the smiles on the faces of the Russians present, it could only be concluded that he had come up with a witty and appropriate toast. As the Americans and British grabbed their glasses, the interpreter rose to say, "Marshal Stalin says the men's room is on the right."

3. *If you are in some position where you are likely to be called on, it is a good idea to have a few short toasts memorized.* A groom at his own wedding banquet was asked to propose a toast to the bride. Unprepared, he got to his feet, put his hand on the bride's shoulder and said, "Ladies and gentlemen, I . . . I don't know what to say. This thing was forced upon me."

4. *Check the context of your toast if it is quoted from a known poem or prose work.* Prince Philip of Great Britain was told the story of the man who toasted him at a banquet with two lines from John Dryden:

A man so various he seemed to be
Not one but all mankind's epitome.

Philip liked the toast and later looked up the remaining lines of the poem:

Stiff in opinions, always in the wrong
Was everything but starts and nothing long;
But in the course of revolving moon
Was chemist, fiddler, statesman and buffoon.

5. *Don't get ahead of yourself.* When Queen Louise of Prussia met the conquering Napoleon, she drank to him with this toast: "To the health and kindness of Napoleon the Great. He has taken our states, and soon will return them to us."

   Napoleon bowed and replied, "Do not drink it all, Madame."

6. *Make sure the toast you are delivering is appropriate to the group and occasion.* "Bottoms up" would be inappropriate at the beginning of a boat race.

7. *Don't push someone into proposing a toast, as the result may not be the one desired.* There are many examples, but a perfect case in point involved Winston Churchill in the 1920s after he had served as First Lord of the Admiralty. At a dinner party, someone pestered him for a toast to the traditions of the Royal Navy. "The traditions of the Royal Navy?" was his response. "I'll give you the traditions of the Royal Navy. Rum, buggery and the lash."

8. *When proposing a toast, make sure you know what you are drinking.* Basic advice, but here's what Rudy Maxa reported on toasting in the nation's capital in the September 1986 *Washingtonian*: "Then there's the story, perhaps apocryphal, about an American military man toasting his Japanese hosts at a Washington dinner party. Mistaking a finger bowl for a goblet, he finished his remarks and drank deeply from the bowl. Not wishing to offend, fellow guests reached for their own finger bowls and followed suit."

9. *Don't drink with Old Saxons.* An Old Saxon toasting custom required that a man draw the sharp edge of his knife across his forehead, letting the blood drip into his wine cup and then drinking a health to the woman he loved.

SEE ALSO: *Secrets; Toastmaster*

HISTORIC

What follows is a small, chronologically displayed museum of special toasts that were tied to a historic place, cause, or event. There are hundreds more, but these are some of the most important. One should also be aware of the fact that certain mottos and rallying cries—"Fifty-four Forty or Fight!" "Remember the Alamo!" "Remember the Maine!" "Keep 'em flying!"—were also toasts in their time.

Love and wine are the bonds that fasten us all,
The world but for these to confusion would fall,
Were it not for the pleasures of love and good wine,
Mankind, for each trifle their lives would resign;
They'd not value dull life nor could live without thinking,
Nor would kings rule the world but for love and good drinking.
—Toast of 1675

Mr. Payne, to err is nature; to rectify error is glory. I believe I was wrong yesterday.
—GEORGE WASHINGTON, 1754. After an argument with a man named William Payne, it had been expected that Washington might challenge the man to a duel. Instead he sent Payne wine and the toast to drink it with.

Some delight in fighting Fields,
Nobler transports Bacchus yields,
Fill the bowl I ever said,
'Tis better to lie drunk than dead.
—Toast of 1766

And he that will this health deny,
Down among the dead men let him lie.
—JOHN DYER, from "Here's a Health to the King," eighteenth century

Here's to the squire who goes on parade,
Here's to the citizen soldier
Here's to the merchant who fights for his trade
Whom danger increasingly makes bolder,
    Let mirth appear,
    Every heart cheer
The toast that I give is to the brave volunteer.
—American Revolution

Freedom from mobs as well as kings.
—American, late eighteenth century

We mutually pledge to each other our lives, our fortunes, and our
sacred honor.
—THOMAS JEFFERSON

When lifting high the rosy glass,
Each comrade toasts his favorite lass
And to his fond bosom near;
Ah, how can I the nectar sip,
Or Anna's name escape my lip
When Mary is my dear?
—Sailor's toast, 1795

Stand to your glasses steady,
    And drink to your comrade's eyes:
Here's a cup to the dead already,
    And hurrah for the next that dies.
—Refrain from a long, morose toast with much lore attached to it.
    Depending on the source, it was a hymn to cholera, the toast of the
    English dying in the Black Hole of Calcutta in 1758, or a pledge of soldiers
    during the first Burmese war. It has been attributed to several authors
    including Alfred Domett and Bartholomew Dowling. During World
    War I, it was used by British and American pilots.

Ladies and Gentlemen, this is the last time I shall drink to
your health as a public man. I do it with all sincerity, wishing
you all possible happiness.
—GEORGE WASHINGTON, March 3, 1797. The day before he retired from
    office, Washington gave a dinner for President-elect John Adams at which
    he raised his glass and gave this toast.

Rum—the greatest undertaker upon earth.
—Early American temperance toast (to be drunk with water)

Ask nothing that is not clearly right and submit to nothing that is
wrong.
—ANDREW JACKSON's motto, often used as a toast in the nineteenth
    century

Here's to an honest man—the noblest work of God.
—ANDREW JACKSON

May we never have a Fox too cunning nor a Pitt too deep.
—English, early nineteenth century. It refers to Charles James Fox and
    William Pitt, the two great political figures.

To the total abolition of the slave trade.
—Abolitionists' toast

May the blackness of heart, not blackness of face, distinguish the free
man from the slave.
—Early abolitionist sentiment. It first appeared in England in 1812 but was
    soon embraced by Americans who opposed slavery.

Up to my lips and down to my hips
The further it goes, the better it gits
Here's peace at home and plenty abroad—
Love your wife and serve the Lord—Drink!
—Toast of the antebellum South

Here's to ye, Mr. Lincoln! May you die both late and aisy,
And when you lie with the top of each toe turned up to the
     roots of the daisy,
May this be your epitaph nately writ:
"Tho' traitors abused him vilely,
He was honest and kind, and loved a joke,
And he pardoned Miles O'Reilly."
—MILES O'REILLY, pseudonym of Charles Graham Halpine, from *Life
   and Adventures, Songs, Services, and Speeches of Private Miles O'Reilly*

I drink to all, whate'er their creed,
     Their country, rank, communion
Who in the cause of Freedom bleed,
     And combat for the Union!
—Union toast

There are bonds of all sorts in this world of ours,
     Letters of friendship and ties of flowers,
     And true lovers' knots I ween;
The girl and boy and bound by a kiss,
But there's never a bond, old friend like this:
     We have drunk from the same canteen!
—GENERAL CHARLES G. HALPINE. This toast was very popular among
   the Union veterans of the Grand Army of the Republic.

Under the sod and the dew,
     Waiting the judgment day;
Love and tears for the blue,
     Tears and love for the gray.
—FRANCIS M. FINCH

Nine times nine cheers!
—Nineteenth-century English toast often directed at Queen Victoria. Over
   time, it became shortened to "Cheers!"

May the New Year grant you
a clean shirt
a clear conscience
and a ticket to California in your pocket.
—Irish, nineteenth century

To the memory of
GEORGE WASHINGTON
The childless father of seventy millions.
—Popular nineteenth-century toast

Solitary and alone in its grandeur stands forth the character of
Washington in history: solitary and alone like some peak that has no
fellow in the mountain range of greatness.
—SENATOR JOHN W. DANIELS of Virginia at the dedication of the
    Washington Monument

Huge and alert, irascible yet strong,
We make our fitful way 'mid right and wrong.
One time we pour out millions to be free,
Then rashly sweep an empire from the sea!
One time we strike the shackles from the slaves,
And then, quiescent, we are ruled by knaves.
Often we rudely break restraining bars,
And confidently reach out toward the stars.

Yet under all there flows a hidden stream
Sprung from the Rock of Freedom, the great dream
Of Washington and Franklin, men of old
Who knew that freedom is not bought with gold.
This is the Land we love, our heritage,
Strange mixture of the gross and fine, yet sage.
And full of promise—destined to be great
Drink to Our Native Land! God Bless the State!
—ROBERT BRIDGES, "A Toast to Our Native Land," late nineteenth
    century

To our country: May her literary men do her honor by speaking the truth, of her and all things; may they give her immortality by making the truth eloquent and beautiful.

—WOODROW WILSON, as president of Princeton, to Lucy Smith of New Orleans in a letter of December 8, 1898

A mighty nation mourns thee yet;
Thy gallant crew—their awful fate;
And justice points her finger straight,
Lest we forget—lest we forget!
—On the sinking of the *Maine*

Home, boys, home! It's home we ought to be!
Home, boys, home! In God's country;
Where the ash and the oak and weeping willow tree
And the grass grows green in North Ameriky!
—Toast of the U.S. Army in the Philippines at the end of the Spanish-American War

Their arms our sure defense,
Our arms, their recompense,
    Fall in!
—Women's toast to men returning from the Spanish-American War

May it always carry messages of happiness.
—On the christening of the cable between San Francisco and Honolulu, December 15, 1902

Here's to the Trusts which are not dead as yet,
For the longer you curse 'em the stronger they get.
So if we would strangle their dragon-like breath
Let's try a new method and bless 'em to death.
—WALLACE IRWIN, 1904

To all who put their trust in God—but never their God in a Trust.

Gentlemen, I believe your victories were won on water.
—WILLIAM JENNINGS BRYAN, when asked to toast the British navy,
which he did with a glass of water

A glass of good Nature's ale—may its recipe never fail.
—Water toast of the anti-saloon forces, early twentieth century. "Nature's
ale," of course, refers to water, as does "Adam's ale."

Ireland—St. Patrick destroyed its creeping things of other days—
may his disciples speedily exterminate the political reptiles of the
present age.
—Irish, early twentieth century

I've burnt the midnight oil, many knotty problems solving;
I've ponder'd o'er human woes, including those involving
The rights of lovely women, to which they cling like leeches;
But, tell me, (for I'm all at sea,
As to what the moral teaches)—
When the dears go out to vote, are they to wear our breeches?
—PAUL LOWE, antisuffragette toast, 1910

See our glorious banner waving,
      Hear the bugle call;
Rally comrades to the standard
      Down with alcohol!
—American nonalcoholic toast, popular among temperance groups, circa 1915

To our women, our horses, and the men who ride them.
—Calvary toast, World War I, from the French

To the automobile: the rich man's wine and the poor man's chaser.

Here's to my car and your car, and may they never meet.

To the confounding of our enemies.
—Toast favored and made popular by Dean Acheson

Here's to today!

For tomorrow we may be radioactive.

—Early atomic age toast

Every president seeks to use the press. The press can take care of itself and hopefully so can a president. I hope that my epitaph will be with relations to the White House press corps, "He gave as good as he got."

—RONALD REAGAN, making his farewell to the White House press corps, April 21, 1988

I would like to propose a toast to a future of peace for the Soviet and the American people and for all nations on earth, to idealism and idealists, to the health of the president of the United States of America, Mr. George Bush, and Barbara Bush, to the health and well-being of all present here, to the happiness of our children and grandchildren.

—MIKHAIL GORBACHEV, at the Russian embassy during the summit in Washington on June 1, 1990

Ladies and gentlemen, I invite all of you to join me in a toast to our gracious hosts, President and Mrs. Gorbachev, to lasting peace, and to this wonderful spirit of freedom.

—GEORGE H. W. BUSH in response to Gorbachev's toast

SEE ALSO: *Alliterative; America; Military; Prohibition; Secrets*

HOME

God bless our mortgaged home.

Here's to home, the place where we are treated best, and grumble the most.

—From an old postcard

Long may your lum reek.*
—ROBERT BURNS

May blessings be upon your house,
 Your roof and hearth and walls;
May there be lights to welcome you
 When evening's shadow
 falls—
The love that like a guiding star
 Still signals when you roam;
A book, a friend—these be the things
 That make a house a home.
—MYRTLE REED, a house blessing

SEE ALSO: *General; Guests; Hosts and Hostesses*

HOSTS AND HOSTESSES

A toast to our host
 And a song from the short and tall of us,
May he live to be
 The guest of all of us!

Here's a health to thine and thee,
 not forgetting mine and me.
When thine and thee again meet mine and me,
may mine and me have as much welcome for thine and thee
as thine and thee have had for mine and me tonight.
—Irish

Here's to our hostess, considerate and sweet;
Her wit is endless, but when do we eat?

---

* Meaning, "Long may your chimney smoke."

I thank you for your welcome,
     which was cordial,
And your cordial, which is
     welcome.

Let's drink to the maker of the
feast, our friend and host. May
his generous heart, like his
good wine, only grow mellower
with the years.

May the roof above us never fall in, and may we friends gathered
below never fall out.
—Irish

May you be Hung, Drawn, and Quartered!
Yes—Hung with diamonds,
Drawn in a coach and four,
And quartered in the best houses in the land.

To our host,
An excellent man;
For is not a man
Fairly judged by the
Company he keeps?

To our host: The rapturous, wild, and ineffable pleasure of drinking at
somebody else's expense.
—HENRY SAMBROOKE LEIGH, 1870

To our hostess! She's a gem. We love her, God bless her.
And the devil take her husband.

To the sun that warmed the vineyard,
     To the juice that turned to wine,
To the host that cracked the bottle,
     And made it yours and mine.

What's a table richly spread
Without a woman at its head?

You are welcome, my fair guests; that noble lady,
Our gentleman, that is not freely merry,
Is not my friend: This to confirm my welcome:
And to you all good health.
—WILLIAM SHAKESPEARE, *Henry VIII*, Act I

SEE ALSO: *Friendship; General; Guests*

HUSBANDS

Here's to the man who loves his wife,
    And loves his wife alone.
For many a man loves another man's wife,
    When he ought to be loving his own.

May your life be long and sunny
And your husband fat and funny.

To my husband: May he never be
tight—but tight or sober, my
husband.

When the husband drinks to the
wife, all would be well; when the
wife drinks to the husband, all is.
—Old English proverb

SEE ALSO: *Alliterative; Anniversaries; Man and Men; Weddings*

INTERNATIONAL

This assembly of short toasts or, as they have been called, cheers should get you through a United Nations reception. Their English equivalents are along the lines of "Cheers," "To your health," and "Bottoms up."

ALBANIAN: Gëzuar.

ARABIAN: Bismillah. Fi schettak.

ARMENIAN: Genatzt.

AUSTRIAN: Prosit.

BELGIAN: Op uw gezonheid.

BRAZILIAN: Saúde. Viva.

CHINESE: Nien Nien nu e. Kong Chien. Kan bei. Yum sen. Wen lie.

CZECH: Na Zdravi. Nazdar.

DANISH: Skål.

DUTCH: Proost. Geluch.

EGYPTIAN: Fee sihetak.

ESPERANTO: Je zia sano.

ESTONIAN: Tervist.

FINNISH: Kippis. Maljanne.

FRENCH: A votre santé. Santé

GERMAN: Prosit. Auf ihr wohl.

GREEK: Eis Igian.

GREENLANDIC: Kasûgta.

HAWAIIAN: Okole maluna. Hauoli maoli oe. Meli kalikama.

HUNGARIAN: Kedves egeszsegere.

ICELANDIC: Santanka nu.

INDIAN: Jaikind. Aanand.

INDONESIAN: Selamat.

IRANIAN: Besalmati. Shemoh.

ITALIAN: A la salute. Salute. Cin cin.

JAPANESE: Kampai. Banzai.

KOREAN: Kong gang ul wi ha yo.

LITHUANIAN: I sveikas.

MALAYAN: Slamat minum.

MEXICAN: Salud.

MOROCCAN: Saha wa'afiab.

NEW ZEALAND: Kia ora.

NORWEGIAN: Skål.

PAKISTANI: Sanda bashi.

PHILIPPINE: Mabuhay.

POLISH: Na zdrowie. Vivat.

PORTUGUESE: A sua saúde.

ROMANIAN: Noroc. Pentru sanatatea dunneavoastra.

RUSSIAN: Na zdorovia.

SPANISH: Salud. Salud, amor, y pesetas y el tiempo para gustarlos! (Health, love, and money and the time to enjoy them!)

SWEDISH: Skål.

THAI: Sawasdi.

TURKISH: Şerefe.

UKRAINIAN: Boovatje zdorovi.

WELSH: Iechyd da.

YUGOSLAVIAN: Zivio.

ZULU: Oogy wawa.

SEE ALSO: *Irish; Latin; Scotch*

IRISH

No area of the world where English is spoken—and probably none where any other language is spoken, for that matter—can compare with Ireland as a stronghold for the custom of toasting. More often than not, toasts go by the name of "blessings" in Ireland. There are large numbers of them, and their use seems to be growing. As the popular Irish writer John B. Keane said in an article on the subject, "Nothing has the grace or the beauty of an old Irish blessing and recently I was delighted to learn that instead of dying out, Irish blessings are on the increase. All you have to do is listen and if you spend a day in the Irish countryside you will go away with countless blessings ringing in your ears."

Blessings are often used beyond the reach of a glass, but all make appropriate toasts. A graveside blessing—"That the devil mightn't hear of his death till he's safe inside the walls of heaven"—can be equally appropriate as a toast to the departed.

The vast majority of toasts in this section (along with others scattered throughout the rest of the book) come from the collection of Jack McGowan of the Irish Distillers International of Dublin, who has gathered them from all over his nation.

One other thing: Many Irish toasts are one-liners that lend themselves to being assembled into longer toasts. This is especially true of the many *May you*'s.

A goose in your garden except on Christmas Day.

Better be quarreling than lonesome.

Health and long life to you.
The wife/husband of your choice to you.
A child every year to you.
Land without rent to you.
And may you be half an hour in heaven
before the devil knows you're dead.
Sláinte!*

Health and long life to you.
The wife/husband of your choice to you.
Land free of rent to you.
From this day forth.

---

* Pronounced *slawn-cheh*; it means Health!

Health to everyone
From the tip of the roof to the side of the fire
From wall to wall
And if there's anyone *in* the wall, speak up!

Here's a health to your enemies' enemies!

Here's that ye may never die nor be kilt till ye break your bones over a bushel of glory.

Here's to a fair price on a fair day.

Here's to eyes in your head and none in your spuds!

Here's to health, peace, and prosperity. May the flower of love never be nipped by the frost of disappointment; nor shadow of grief fall among a member of this circle.

Here's to the land of the shamrock so green,
Here's to each lad and his darling colleen,
Here's to the ones we love dearest and most,
And may God save old Ireland—that's an Irishman's toast.

Here's to you, _____. When God measures you, may he put the tape around your big and generous heart and not around your small and foolish head.

Here's to your health
May God bring you luck
And may your journey be smooth and happy.

It is not a sin not to be Irish, but it is a great shame.
—SEAN O'HUIGINN, former consul general of Ireland

May meat always sweeten your pot.

May the day keep fine for you.

May the devil say a prayer for you.

May the enemies of Ireland never meet a friend.

May the frost never afflict your spuds.
May the outside leaves of your cabbage always be free from worms.
May the crows never pick your haystack and may your
    donkey always be in foal.

May the horns of your cattle touch heaven.

May the path to hell grow green for lack of travelers.

May the road rise to meet you.
May the wind be always at your back,
the sun shine warm upon your face,
the rain fall soft upon your fields.
And until we meet again,
may God hold you in the hollow of His hand.

May the rocks in your field turn to gold.

May the saints protect you,
And sorrow neglect you,
And bad luck to the one
That doesn't respect you.

May the ship that took your sons away
to farm the Californias
bring home a harvest of riches for Christmas.

May the swallows be first in your eaves.
May your milk never turn.
May your horses never stray.
May your hens always lay.
May lean bacon hang from your rafters.

May the thatch on your house
be as strong as the thatch on your head;
May the moon be as full as your glass
and American dollars arrive in the post by Christmas.

May there always be work for your hands to do.
May your purse always hold a coin or two.
May the sun always shine on your windowpane.
May a rainbow be certain to follow each rain.
May the hand of a friend always be near you.
May God fill your heart with gladness to cheer you.

May time never turn your head gray.

May those who love us love us;
And those that don't love us,
May God turn their hearts;
And if He doesn't turn their hearts,
May He turn their ankles,
So we'll know them by their limping.

May we all be alive this time in twelve months.

May what goes down not come back up again.

May you always wear silk.

May you be seven times better off a year from now.

May you die in bed at ninety-five years, shot by a jealous husband/wife.

May you have nicer legs than yours under the table before the new spuds are up.
—A toast for the bachelor

May you have the hindsight to know where you've been, the foresight to know where you're going, and the insight to know when you're going too far.

May you have warm words on a cold evening,
A full moon on a dark night,
And the road downhill all the way to your door.

May you look back on the past with as much pleasure as you look forward to the future.

May you never give cherries to pigs or advice to a fool nor praise the green corn till you've seen the ripe field.

May you never have to eat your hat.

May you never make an enemy
when you could make a friend
unless you meet a fox among your chickens.

May your blessings outnumber
the shamrocks that grow,
and may trouble avoid you
wherever you go.

May your fire be as warm as the weather is cold.

May your fire never go out.

May your shadow never grow less.

May your well never run dry.

No wasps near your honey, but bees in your hive.

That the ten toes of your feet might always steer you
clear of misfortune, and I hope,
before you're much older,
that you'll hear much better toasts than this.
    Sláinte!

The Irish heart—quick and strong in its generous impulses,
firm in its attachments, sound to the core.

To a warm bed, a dry stook,* and glass in your window.

To the thirst that is yet to come.

To the three skills of a hare:
sharp turning,
high jumping,
and strong running against the hill.

To twenty years a growing
twenty years at rest
twenty years declining
and twenty years when it doesn't matter
whether we're there or not.

To warm words on a cold day.

Wert thou all that I wish thee,
Great, glorious and free,
First flower of the earth,
And first gem of the sea.
—Thomas Moore

---

* A stook is a sheaf of grain.

Your Health! May we have one together in ten years time
and a few in between.

SEE ALSO: *Babies and Children; Birthdays; Bulls; Christmas; Death;
Food; Health; Historic; Hosts and Hostesses; New Year's; St. Patrick's Day;
Weddings*

JEWISH

The prime Jewish toast is the Hebrew *L'chayim*, which means "to life," or "to
your health." *Mazel tov* is also used as a toast. Leo Rosten explains which to
use when in his *Joys of Yiddish*: "Some innocents confuse *L'chayim* with *mazel tov*, using one when the other would be appropriate. There is no reason to
err. *L'chayim* is used whenever one would say 'Your health,' 'Cheers!' or (I
shudder to say) 'Here's mud in your eye.' *Mazel tov!* is used as 'Congratu-
lations.'"

LATIN

Ad finem esto fidelis. (Be faithful to the end.)

Amor patriae. (The love of our country.)

Carpe diem. (Seize the day.)

Carpe noctem. (Seize the night.)

Dilige amicos. (Love your friends.)

Dum vivimus vivamus. (Let us live while we live.)

Esto perpetua. (Be thou perpetual.)

Pro aris et focis. (For our altars and fireside.)

Propino tibi. (I drink to you.)

Vox populi vox Dei. (The voice of the people is the voice of God.)

LIBATIONS

A drink, my lass, in a deep clear glass,
Just properly tempered by ice,
And here's to the lips mine have kissed,
And if they were thine, here's twice.

A glass in the hand's worth two on the shelf—
Tipple it down and refresh yourself!

A small glass and thirsty!
Be sure never ask it:
Man might as well serve up
His soup in a basket.
—LEIGH HUNT

A toast to any gentleman
So shrewd and diplomatic
Who never—though he's in his
        cups—
Decides he's operatic!

At the punch bowl's brink
Let the thirsty think
What they say in Japan:
"First the man takes a drink,
Then the drink takes a drink,
Then the drink takes the man!"

Better to pay the tavernkeeper than the druggist.
—Spanish

Come, friends, come let us drink again,
This liquid from the nectar vine,
For water makes you dumb and stupid,
Learn this from the fishes—
They cannot sing, nor laugh, nor drink
This beaker full of sparkling wine.
—Old Dutch song

Drink and be merry, for our time on earth is short, and death lasts forever.

Drink, for you know not
      When you came, nor why,
Drink, for you know not why
      You go, nor whence.
—OMAR KHAYYÁM

Drink today and drown all sorrow,
You shall perhaps not do't tomorrow
Best while you have it, use your breath;
There is no drinking after death.
—FRANCIS BEAUMONT and JOHN FLETCHER, *The Blood Brother*

Drink with impunity—
Or anyone who happens to invite you!
—ARTEMUS WARD

Fill the bumper fair;
      Every drop we sprinkle
O'er the brow of care,
      Smooths away a wrinkle.
—THOMAS MOORE

Fill up the goblet, let it swim
In foam, that overlooks the brim;
He that drinks deepest, here's to him.
—CHARLES COTTON

Hath thy ale virtue or thy beer strength, that the tongue of man may
be tickled and his palate pleased in the morning.
—BEN JONSON

He who goes to bed, and goes to bed sober,
Falls as the leaves do, and dies in October;
But he who goes to bed, and does so mellow,
Lives as he ought to, and dies a good fellow.
—Parody of Beaumont and Fletcher's toast from *The Blood Brother*

Here is a toast to all the toasts,
 As toasted they should be,
Given by paupers, kings, and hosts,
 With much felicity.

It flies o'er mountains, swims the sea,
 Tunnels the earth below,
Spreading conviviality
 Wherever it doth go.

It is not great, nor is it small,
 Is neither far nor near.
A well-considered wish from all,
 "Another bottle here."
—JAMES MONROE MCLEAN, *The Book of Wine*

Here's may we never drink worse!

Here's to the bottle which holds a store
Of imprisoned joy and laughter!
    Here's to this bottle,
    Many more bottles,
And others to follow after.

Here's to the four cardinal sins of man
—stealing, lying, swearing, and drinking.
When you steal, steal away from dull companions;
when you lie, lie to protect a lovely lady;
when you swear, swear by your country;
and when you drink, drink with me.
—JACK LONDON, to a group of publishers in New York City, 1903

Here's to the man who takes the pledge,
Who keeps his word and does not hedge,
Who won't give up and won't give in
Till the last man's out and there's no more gin.

Here's to the temperance supper,
    With water in glasses tall,
And coffee and tea to end with—
    And me not there at all.

Here's to water, the best of things that man to man can bring. But
who am I, that I should have the best of everything?

Here's to you that makes me wear old clothes;
Here's to you that turns my friends to foes,
But seeing you're so near—here goes!
Here it goes under my nose—
God knows I need it.

Ho, gentlemen! Lift your glasses up,
Each gallant, each swain and lover;
A kiss to the beads that brim in the cup,
A laugh for the foam spilt over.

Honor, love, fame, wealth may desert us, but thirst is eternal.

I drink no more than a sponge.
—François Rabelais

I drink to your health when I'm with you,
I drink to your health when I'm alone,
I drink to your health so often
I'm beginning to worry about my own.

I drink when I have occasion and sometimes when I have no occasion.
—Miguel De Cervantes

If all be true as we do think
There are five reasons why we drink:
Good wine, a Friend, or being Dry
Or lest one should be, by and by . . .
Or any other reason why!
—Henry Aldrich, dean of Christ Church, circa 1620

In an honest tavern let me die,
Before my lips a brimmer lie,
And angel choirs come down and cry,
"Peace to thy soul, my jolly boy."
—Walter Map

Kings it makes gods, and meaner creatures, kings.
—William Shakespeare, *King Richard III*, Act V

Let Princes revel at the pump, let peers with ponds make free;
But whiskey, wine, and even beer, is good enough for me.

Let schoolmasters puzzle their brain
With grammar and nonsense and learning;
Good liquor, I stoutly maintain,
Gives genius a better discerning.
—Oliver Goldsmith

"Lips that touch liquor shall never touch mine";
Thus cried the maiden with fervor divine;
But from her statement what must we infer—
They shan't touch her liquor, or shan't touch her?
—PUCK in William Shakespeare's *A Midsummer Night's Dream*

May the beam of the glass never destroy the ray of the mind.

May the bloom of the face never extend to the nose.

May the tears of the tankard afford us relief.

May you ever have lived—
       May you ever have loved—
So that good drink—
       Will never make you think—
You might have done better.

Mingle with the friendly bowl,
The feast of reason and the flow of soul.
—ALEXANDER POPE

Now here's to Addition—
       Another pint, pray!
Then here's to Subtraction—
       Take th' old one away!
Here's Multiplication—
       So double the wine!
And here's to Division—
       That's yours, and this mine!
—WALLACE RICE

O Water! Pure, free of pollution
I vainly wished that I dared trust it.
But I've an iron constitution,
And much I fear that water'd rust it.
—W. E. P. FRENCH

Observe, when Mother Earth is dry,
    She drinks the droppings of the sky,
And then the dewy cordial gives
    To every thirsty plant that lives.

The vapors which at evening sweep
    Are beverage to the swelling deep,
And when the rosy sun appears,
    He drinks the misty ocean's tears.

The moon, too, quaffs her paly stream
    of luster from the solar beam;
Then hence with all your sober thinking!
    Since Nature's holy law is drinking,
I'll make the law of Nature mine,
    And pledge the Universe in wine.
—THOMAS MOORE, "The Universal Toast"

One sip of this will bathe the drooping spirits in delight beyond the bliss of dreams.
—JOHN MILTON

One swallow doesn't make a summer, but it breaks a New Year's resolution.

Take the glass away:—
I know I hadn't oughter:—
I'll take a pledge—I will—
I never will drink water.
—W. E. P. FRENCH

The corkscrew—a useful key to unlock the storehouse of wit, the treasury of laughter, the front door of fellowship, and the gate of pleasant folly.
—W. E. P. FRENCH

The first glass for myself; the second for my friends; the third for good
humor, and the fourth for mine enemies.
—Sir William Temple, first quoted in the *Spectator* by Joseph Addison,
    October 13, 1711

The man that isn't jolly after drinking
Is just a driveling idiot, to my thinking.
—Euripides

Then fill the cup, fill high! fill high!
    Nor spare the rosy wine,
If death be in the cup, we'll die—
    Such death would be divine.
—James Russell Lowell

There are several reasons for drinking,
And one has just entered my head;
If a man cannot drink when he's living
How the hell can he drink when he's dead?

There's naught, no doubt, so much the spirit calms as rum and true
religion.
—Lord Byron

'Tis a pity wine should be so deleterious,
For tea and coffee leave us much more serious.
—Lord Byron

Too much is plenty.
—Joseph M. Weber and Lew Fields

Within this goblet, rich and deep,
I cradle all my woes to sleep.
—Thomas Moore

SEE ALSO: *Beer and Ale; Biblical; Champagne; Mornings After; Prohibition; Revelry; Spirits (Ardent); Wine*

LIMERICKS

There is an old tradition among those who collect limericks of using them as toasts. All one has to do is change the limerick's original first few words to "Here's to . . ." For example:

Here's to a lady from Guam
Who said, "Now the ocean's so calm
    I will swim, for a lark."
    She encountered a shark.
Let us now sing the ninetieth psalm.

Here's to a young woman named Bright,
Whose speed was much faster than light.
    She set out one day,
    In a relative way,
And returned on the previous night.

Here's to the young lady from Oak Knoll
Who thought it exceedingly droll
    At a masquerade ball
    Wearing nothing at all
To back in as a Parker House roll.

LOVE

A Book of Verses underneath the Bough,
A Jug of Wine, a Loaf of Bread—and Thou
    Beside me singing in the Wilderness—
Oh, Wilderness were Paradise enow!
—EDWARD FITZGERALD, from *The Rubáiyát of Omar Khayyám*

Because I love you truly,
Because you love me, too,
My very greatest happiness
Is sharing life with you.

Brew me a cup for a winter's night.
For the wind howls loud and the furies fight;
Spice it with love and stir it with care,
And I'll toast your bright eyes, my sweetheart fair.
—MINNA THOMAS ANTRIM

Come in the evening, or come in the morning,
Come when you are looked for, or come without warning,
A thousand welcomes you will find here before you,
And the oftener you come here, the more I'll adore you.
—Irish

Come live with me, and be my love,
And we will all the pleasures prove,
That valleys, groves, or hills, or fields,
Or woods and steepy mountains yield.
—CHRISTOPHER MARLOWE, "Passionate Shepherd to His Love"

Do you love me
Or do you not?
You told me once
But I forgot.

Give me a kisse, and to that kisse a score;
Then to that twenty, adde a hundred more;
A thousand to that hundred; so kiss on,
To make that thousand up a million;
Treble that million, and when that is done,
Let's kisse afresh, as when we first begun.
—ROBERT HERRICK, "To Anthea," in *Hesperides*

Here's to Dan Cupid, the little squirt,
He's lost his pants, he's lost his shirt,
He's lost most everything but his aim,
Which shows that love is a losing game.

Here's to fertility—the toast of agriculture and the bane of love.

Here's to love and unity,
Dark corners and opportunity.

Here's to love, that begins with a fever and ends with a yawn.

Here's to love—with its billets-doux, bills and coos, biliousness, bills,
and bills of divorcement.

Here's to one and only one,
    And may that one be he
Who loves but one and only one,
    And may that one be me.

Here's to the land we love and the love we land.

Here's to the maid who is thrifty,
And knows it is folly to yearn,
And picks out a lover of fifty,
Because he has money to burn.

Here's to the pictures on my desk. May they never meet.

Here's to the prettiest, here's to the wittiest,
Here's to the truest of all who are true,
Here's to the neatest one, here's to the sweetest one,
Here's to them all in one—here's to you.

Here's to the wings of love—
   May they never molt a feather;
Till my big boots and your little shoes
   Are under the bed together.

Here's to the woman that I love
And here's to the woman that loves me,
And here's to all those that love her that I love,
And to those that love her that love me.

Here's to this water,
   Wishing it were wine
Here's to you, my darling,
   Wishing you were mine.

Here's to those who love us,
   And here's to those who don't,
A smile for those who are willing to,
   And a tear for those who won't.

Here's to those who'd love us
   If we only cared;
Here's to those we'd love,
   If we only dared.

Here's to you who halves my sorrows and doubles my joys.

I drink to your charm, your beauty and your brains—which gives you
a rough idea of how hard up I am for a drink.
—GROUCHO MARX

I have known many,
   liked a few,
Loved one—
   Here's to you!

I love you more than yesterday, less than tomorrow.

I would be friends with you and have your love.

If I were I, and you were you, would you?
There are times I would and times I wouldn't,
Times that I could and times I couldn't;
But the times I could and would and I felt game
Are the times I'm with you, dear.

If we cannot love unconditionally, love is already in a critical
condition.
—Johann Wolfgang von Goethe

It warms me, it charms me,
To mention but her name,
It heats me, it beats me,
And sets me a' on flame.
—Robert Burns

Let us be gay while we may
And seize love with laughter
I'll be true as long as you
But not for a moment after.

Let's drink to love,
Which is nothing—
Unless it's divided by two.

Love, and you shall be loved. All love is mathematically just, as much
as the two sides of an algebraic equation.
—Ralph Waldo Emerson

Love doesn't make the world go 'round. Love is what makes the ride
worthwhile.
—Franklin P. Jones

Love is what you've been through with somebody.
—James Thurber

Love makes time pass—
Time makes love pass.

May love draw the curtain and friendship the cork.

May those now love
Who never loved before.
May those who've loved
Now love the more.

May we kiss those we please
And please those we kiss.

May we love as long as we live, and live as long as we love.

Mutual love, the crown of bliss.
—JOHN MILTON

Mystery and disappointment are not absolutely indispensable to the growth of love, but they are often very powerful auxiliaries.
—CHARLES DICKENS, *Nicholas Nickleby*

Say it with flowers
    Say it with eats,
Say it with kisses,
    Say it with sweets,
Say it with jewelry,
    Say it with drink,
But always be careful
    Not to say it with ink.

The love you give away is the only love you keep.
—ELBERT HUBBARD

They say there's microbes in a kiss,
This rumor is most rife,
Come lady dear, and make of me an invalid for life.

Thou hast no faults, or I no faults can spy;
Thou art all beauty, or all blindness I.

To each man's best and truest love—unless it be himself.

To every lovely lady bright,
I wish a gallant faithful knight;
To every faithful lover, too,
I wish a trusting lady true.
—Sir Walter Scott

We'll drink to love. Love, the one irresistible force that annihilates distance, caste, prejudice, and principles. Love, the pastime of the Occident, the passion of the East. Love, that stealeth upon us like a thief in the night, robbing us of rest, but bestowing in its place a gift more precious than the sweetest sleep. Love is the burden of my toast—here's looking at you.

Were't the last drop in the well,
    As I gasped upon the brink,
Ere my fainting spirit fell,
    'Tis to thee I would drink.
—Lord Byron

Yesterday's yesterday while to-day's here,
To-day is to-day till to-morrow appear;
To-morrow's to-morrow until to-day's past—
And kisses are kisses as long as they last.
—Oliver Herford

SEE ALSO: *Alliterative; Anniversaries; Celia's Toast (with Variations); General; Lust; Weddings*

LUCK

A jolly good smoke, a nicely turned joke,
A handful of trumps when at play;
A drop of old wine, champagne that's fine,
And a run of good luck from today.

As you slide down the banister of life
May the splinters never face the
      wrong way.

Everything of fortune but her
      instability.

Good luck till we are tired of it.

I give you play days, heydays, and
paydays!

May Dame Fortune ever smile on you;
      But never her daughter—
      Miss Fortune.

May the chicken never be hatched that will scratch on your
grave.

May we ever be able to part with our troubles to advantage.

May your luck be like the capital of Ireland, "always Dublin."

May your luck ever spread, like jelly on bread.

No amount of planning can ever replace dumb luck!

Stately galleons there are,
    Laden deep with yellow gold;
Treasure argosies from far,
    Jewelled riches in their hold;
May they find a lucky star,
    Captains staunch, and sailors
    bold,
Not a storm or shoal to bar,
    Not a blast of chill or cold
Till safe harbor they shall win—
Thus may all your ships come in!
—OLIVER MARBLE

Then welcome, stranger, cheer be thine,
If thou art a friend, of a friend of mine,
Here's luck . . .
—JAMES MONROE MCLEAN, *The Book of Wine*

To my friend—luck 'til the end!

SEE ALSO: *Better Times; Friendship; General; Irish*

LUST

Here's to Eve—mother of our race;
Who wore a fig leaf in just the right place.
And here's to Adam—daddy of us all;
Who was Johnny-on-the-spot,
When the leaves began to fall.

Here's to lying lips,
Though lying lips are bores,
But lying lips are mighty sweet
When they lie next to yours!

Here's to the game they call Ten Toes;
It's played all over town.
The girls all play with ten toes up,
The boys with ten toes down.

Here's to the girl who lives on the hill.
She won't but her sister will.
So here's to her sister.

Here's to the Hereafter.
If you're not here after
What I'm here after—
You'll be here a long time
After I'm gone.

Here's to the night I met you.
If I hadn't met you, I wouldn't have let you.
Now that I've let you, I'm glad that I met you.
And I'll let you again, I bet you!

Here's to you and here's to me.
And here's to the girl with the well-shaped knee.
Here's to the man with his hand on her garter;
He hasn't got far yet, but he's a damn good starter.

Here's to you, so sweet and good.
God made you; I wish I could.

Hogamus higamus
Men are polygamous
Higamous hogamus
Women monogamous.

It gives me great pleasure.
—GEORGE BERNARD SHAW, when asked to give a toast on the subject of
    sex at a dinner party

Sex: The pleasure is momentary; the expense is exorbitant; the
position ridiculous.
—G. K. CHESTERTON

The ocean is wide;
The sea is level.
Come to my arms
You little devil!

To your genitalia,
May they never jail-a-ya.
—University of Texas, 1950s

Today's the day,
Tonight's the night,
We've shot the stork—
So you're all right!

SEE ALSO: *Love; Revelry; Special Occasions*

MAN AND MEN

Here's to man—he is like a coal-oil lamp; he is not especially bright;
he is often turned down; he generally smokes; and he frequently goes
out at night.

Here's to that most provoking man
The man of wisdom deep
Who never talks when he takes his rest
But only smiles in his sleep.

Here's to the man that kisses his wife
And kisses his wife alone.
For there's many a man kisses another man's wife
When he ought to be kissing his own.

And here's to the man who kisses his child
And kisses his child alone.
For there's many a man kisses another man's child
When he thinks he is kissing his own.

Here's to you, mister,
Whoever you may be.
For you're just the man of the evening,
And nothing more to me.

But, if you and your liquor should conquer,
And I fail to stand the test;
Well, here's to your technique, mister,
I hope it's better than the rest.

I'll drink to the gentleman who I think
Is most entitled to it;
For if anyone ever can drive me to drink
He certainly can do it.

Man is somewhat like a sausage,
Very smooth upon the skin;
But you can never tell exactly
How much hog there is within.

Man is the only animal that laughs, drinks when he is not thirsty, and
makes love at all seasons of the year.
—VOLTAIRE

Men are like candles,
They gleam and are bright,
Men are like candles,
They shine best at night,
Men are like candles,
They sputter about,
And when they are needed
The darn things go out.
—*Charley Jones' Laugh Book*, May 1952

Oh, here's to the good, and the bad men, too
For without them saints would have nothing to do!
Oh, I love them both, and I love them well,
But which I love better, I can never tell.

One must not become attached to animals: they do not last long
enough. Or to men: they last too long.

The man we love: He who thinks most good and speaks less ill of his
neighbor.

The men that women marry,
And why they marry them, will always be
A marvel and a mystery to the world.
—Henry Wadsworth Longfellow

There is more felicity on the far side of baldness than young men can possibly imagine.
—Logan Pearsall Smith

To Man: He is mad; he cannot make a worm, and yet he will be making gods by dozens.
—Montaigne

To the men I've loved
To the men I've kissed
My heartfelt apologies
To the men I've missed!

Women's faults are many,
Men have only two—
Everything they say,
And everything they do.

SEE ALSO: *General; Husbands; Love; Lust; Parents; Weddings*

MILITARY

The most common American military toast is the U.S. Army's "How!" or, sometimes, "Here's how!" It has been in use for more than a hundred years. Several stories of its origin exist: (1) It comes from the Sioux *How kola*, which means "Hello, friend"; (2) it dates to the Boxer Rebellion and the Chinese *Hao!*; (3) it is a spoken symbol for water (H_2O) and whiskey (W), from which the "2" has been dropped.

Traditionally, the navy has stressed a greater variety in its toasts, as the following collection shows.

A stout ship, a clear sea, and a far-off coast in stormy weather.
—Navy

Foes well tarred, and tars well feathered.
—Navy

Good ships, fair winds, and brave seamen.
—Navy

Grog, grub, and glory.
—Navy

Here's to bombers, may they get slower. And here's to fighter planes, may they grow swifter.
—CHARLES A. LINDBERGH, Berlin, July 1936 (quoted in *Lindbergh*, by Leonard Mosley)

Here's to the ships of our navy
And the ladies of our land;
May the first be ever well rigged,
And the latter ever well manned.
—Navy

I give you muscles of steel, nerves of iron, tongues of silver, hearts of gold, necks of leather.
—Marines

Lots of beef and oceans of grog.
—Navy

May no son of the ocean be devoured by his mother.
—Navy

May rudders govern, and ships obey.
—Navy

Put out the red flag, and take ammunition on board.
—REAR ADMIRAL ROBLEY D. EVANS

Put your trust in God, boys, and keep your powder dry.
—COLONEL BLACKER

Some wine, ho!
And let me the canakin clink, clink;
    And let me the canakin clink:
    A soldier's a man,
A life's but a span; Why then, let a soldier drink.
—WILLIAM SHAKESPEARE, *Othello*, Act III

The three generals in peace: General Peace, General Plenty, and General Satisfaction.
—Army

To the militia: Invincible in peace; invisible in war.

The wind that blows, the ship that goes, and the lass that loves a sailor.
—Navy

To a ten-inch gun: In life's great drama may you never play the part for which you have been cast.

True hearts and sound bottoms.
—Navy

SEE ALSO: *America; Historic*

MORNINGS AFTER

"A wet night maketh a dry morning,"
Quoth Hendyng, "rede ye right;
And the cure most fair is the self-same hair
Of the dog that gave the bit."
—"PUNDERSON"

Here's to the good time I must have had!

I wish that my room had a floor
I don't care so much for a door
But this walking around
Without touching the ground
Is getting to be quite a bore.
—GELETT BURGESS

If you'd known when you've enough
Of the punch and the claret cup
It's time you quit the blessed stuff
When you fall down and can't get up.

Lord, how my head aches! What a head have I!
It beats as it would fall in twenty pieces.
—WILLIAM SHAKESPEARE, *Romeo and Juliet*, Act II

MACDUFF: What three things does drink especially provoke?
PORTER: Marry, sir, nose-painting, sleep, and urine.
—WILLIAM SHAKESPEARE, *Macbeth*, Act II

Not drunk is he who from the floor
Can rise again and drink some more;
But drunk is he who prostrate lies,
And who can neither drink nor rise.
—EUGENE FIELD

See the wine in the bowl, how it sparkles tonight.
Tell us what can compete with that red sea of light
Which breathes forth a perfume that deadens all sorrow,
And leaves us blessed now, with a headache tomorrow?
—DR. DORAN

Sing a song of sick gents,
Pockets full of rye,
Four and twenty highballs,
We wish that we might die.

The cocktail is a pleasant drink,
It's mild and harmless, I don't think.
When you've had one, you call for two,
And then you don't care what you do!
Last night I hoisted twenty-three
Of these arrangements into me.
My wealth increased, I swelled with pride,
I was pickled, primed, and ossified;
But R-E-M-O-R-S-E!
The water wagon is the place for me.
I think that somewhere in the game.
I wept and told my real name.
At four I sought my whirling bed;
At eight I woke with such a head!
It is no time for mirth or laughter—
The cold, gray dawn of the morning after.
—GEORGE ADE, from "R-E-M-O-R-S-E," in *The Sultan of Sulu*

NEW YEAR'S

A song for the old, while its knell is tolled,
    And its parting moments fly!
But a song and a cheer for the glad New Year,
    While we watch the old year die!
—GEORGE COOPER

Another year is dawning! Let it be
For better or for worse, another year with thee.

As we start the New Year,
Let's get down on our knees
to thank God we're on our feet.
—Irish

Be at war with your vices, at peace with your neighbors, and let every new year find you a better man.
—Benjamin Franklin

Here's to the bright New Year
    And a fond farewell to the old;
Here's to the things that are yet to come
    And to the memories that we hold.

Here's to you a New Year's toast
May your joy ne'er see a sorrow's ghost.

In the New Year,
may your right hand always be stretched out in friendship,
but never in want.
—Irish

In the year ahead,
May we treat our friends with kindness
and our enemies with generosity.

Let us resolve to do the best we can with what we've got.
—William Feather

May all your troubles during the coming year be as short as your New Year's resolutions.

May it be the best year yet for you, and everything prosper you may do.

May the best of this year be the worst of next.

May the Lord keep you in his hand and never close his fist too tight on you. And may the face of every good news and the back of every bad news be toward us in the New Year.
—Irish

May the New Year bring summer in its wake.
—Irish

May the New Year grant you
the eye of a blacksmith on a nail
the good humor of a girl at a dance
the strong hand of a priest on his parish.
—Irish

May the New Year help to make us old.

May this sweetest old-time greeting
    Heavily laden with good cheers
Bring content, and peace and plenty
    Enough to last through all the year.

May your nets be always full—
your pockets never empty.
May your horse not cast a shoe
nor the devil look at you
in the coming year.
—Irish

Ring out the old, ring in the new,
Ring happy bells across the snow;
The year is going, let him go.
—Alfred, Lord Tennyson

Should auld acquaintance be forgot,
    And never brought to min',
Should auld acquaintance be forgot
    And days of auld lang syne.
For auld lang syne, my dear,
    For auld lang syne,
We'll tak' a cup o' kindness yet,
    For auld lang syne.

And here's a hand, my trusty fierce,
    And gie's a hand o' thine,
And we'll tak' a right guid willie-waught,
    For auld lang syne.
For auld lang syne, my dear,
    For auld lang syne,
We'll tak' a cup o' kindness yet,
    For auld lang syne.

And surely ye'll be your pint stowpt,
    And surely I'll be mine,
And we'll tak' a cup o' kindness yet,
    For auld lang syne.
For auld lang syne, my dear,
    For auld lang syne,
We'll tak' a cup o' kindness yet,
    For auld lang syne.
—ROBERT BURNS

Stir the eggnog, lift the toddy,
Happy New Year, everybody.
—PHYLLIS MCGINLEY

The New Year is ringing in,
May he be bringing in
The good times we've waited for so long in vain!
Without the demanding
All rise and drink standing,
And so say we all of us again and again.

The Old Man's dead. He was okay, maybe.
But here's a health to the brand-new baby.
I give you 20__.

To a firm hand for a flighty beast
an old dog for the long road
a kettle of fish for Friday
and a welcome for the New Year.
—Irish

Welcome be ye that are here,
Welcome all, and make good cheer,
Welcome all, another year.

Whatever you resolve to do,
    On any New Year's Day,
Resolve to yourself to be true
    And live—the same old way.
—New Year's resolution

ODD CUSTOMS

Many old toasting customs (such as drinking out of the skull of a fallen enemy) are impractical today, but here are three that you can still get away
with.

There have always been drinking games and challenges in which the loser
must forfeit a glass—that is, have another drink. The following example
comes from the very old English custom of drinking *super negulum*, or "on the
nail." The drinker must leave just the right amount of beer in his glass so that
when it is poured out, it just covers his fingernail. If too much or too little beer
is left, the penalty is to drink another glass.

Here's a health to Tom Brown,
Let the glass go round,
Drink up your ale without shrinking,
Put a pond on your nail,
And kiss the glass's tail,
And fill it up again without ceasing.

The Romans started the custom in which men drank to the health of their women by having a drink for each letter of the women's names. This has been translated into modern terms:

Three cups to Amy, four to Kate be given,
To Susan five, six Rachel, Bridget seven.

Or, for the opposite sex:

It was not my plan to go on a bender,
But I just left Al for Alexander.

An old tavern amusement (with appropriate instructions):

This is my top. [Clink the top edges of the glasses.]
This is my bottom. [Clink the lower edges.]
And if you're nice to me,
I'll give you a little. [Pour some of your drink into the other person's glass.]

SEE ALSO: *A Selected Glossary of Toast and Tipple; Tongue Twisters; Ultimate Toasts*

OLD THINGS

I drink as the fates ordain it.
    Come fill it and have done with rhymes.
Fill up the lovely glass and drain it
    In memory of dear old times.
—WILLIAM MAKEPEACE THACKERAY

I love everything that's old—old friends, old times, old manners, old books, old wine.
—OLIVER GOLDSMITH

Old wine is wholesomest, old pippins toothsomest,
Old wood burns brightest, old linen washes whitest,
Old soldiers' sweethearts are surest and old lovers are soundest.
—JOHN WEBSTER

Old wood to burn, old wine to drink, old friends to trust, and old
authors to read.
—FRANCIS BACON

SEE ALSO: *Age*

PARENTS

Father. May the love and respect we express toward him make up, at
least in part, for the worry and care we have visited upon him.

He didn't tell me how to live;
he lived,
and let me watch him do it.
—CLARENCE BUDINGTON KELLAND

Here's to the happiest hours of my life—
Spent in the arms of another man's wife;
My mother!

To Life: The first half is ruined by our parents and the second half by
our children.

To Mother and Dad on their wedding anniversary:
    We never know the love of our parents
    for us till we have become parents.
—HENRY WARD BEECHER

To Mother—may she live long enough to forget what fiends we used to be.

You may have a friend,
you may have a lover,
but don't forget,
your best friend is your mother.
—Traditional autograph album inscription

PARTING

Farewell! a word that must be, and hath been—
A sound which makes us linger; yet—farewell.
—LORD BYRON

Friendly may we part and quickly meet again.

Happy are we met, happy have we been,
Happy may we part, and happy meet again.

Here's to good-byes—that they never be spoken!
Here's to friendships—may they never be broken!

It's hard for you-uns and we-uns;
It's hard for we-uns to part;
It's hard for you-uns and we-uns,
'Cause you-uns has we-uns's heart.

May we always part with regret and meet again with pleasure.

Must we part?
Well, if we must—we must—
And in that case
The less said the better.
—RICHARD B. SHERIDAN, *The Critic*, Act II

The pain of parting is nothing to the joy of meeting again.
—CHARLES DICKENS

'Tis grievous parting with good company.
—GEORGE ELIOT

True friendship's laws are by this rule express'd:
Welcome the coming, speed the parting guest.
—ALEXANDER POPE, *The Odyssey of Homer*, Book XIII

SEE ALSO: *Friendship*

PAST, PRESENT, AND FUTURE

Don't worry about the future,
    The present is all thou hast,
The future will soon be present,
    And the present will soon be past.

Every day should be passed
As though it were to be our last.

Here's to the present—and to hell with the past!
A health to the future and joy to the last!

May we always look forward with pleasure, and backward with regret.

The cares of the day, old moralists say,
Are quite enough to perplex one;
Then drive today's sorrow away till tomorrow,
And then put it off till the next one.
—CHARLES DICKENS

The have-beens, the are-nows—and the may-bes!

Then fill the bowl—away with care,
    Our joy shall always last—
Our hopes shall brighten days to come,
    And memory gild the past.
—THOMAS MOORE

This is the best day the world has ever seen.
Tomorrow will be better.
—R. A. CAMPBELL

SEE ALSO: *Age; Anniversaries; Parting; Weddings*

PROFESSIONAL AND OCCUPATIONAL

AGRICULTURE

Aye, the corn, the Royal Corn,
Within whose yellow heart
There is health and strength for all the nations.
—GOVERNOR R. J. OGLESBY of Illinois

Blessed be Agriculture! If one does not have too much of it.
—CHARLES DUDLEY WARNER

Fat cattle, green fields, and many a bushel in your barn.
—Irish

God speed the plough,
But keep me from the handles!
—Yorkshire toast

Good luck to the hoof and the horn
Good luck to the flock and the fleece
Good luck to the growers of corn
With blessings of plenty and peace.

May we spring up like vegetables, have turnip-noses, radish cheeks,
and carroty hair, and may our hearts never be hard, like those of
cabbages, nor may we be rotten at the core.

Some people tell us there ain't no hell,
But they never farmed, so how can they tell?*

Success to the farmers of America—may they always reap a golden
harvest.

To Farmers—founders of civilization.
—Daniel Webster

BAKING
May we never be done so much as to make us crusty.

BARBERING
He cuts our hair
And shaves our face,
And talks and talks
With ease and grace.

BUSINESS
A man should be honest and upright and true—
    No divvy nor graft nor dishonest intent;
But unless he's a chump who cannot catch on
    He'll find out a way to make thirty percent.
—M. Quad (Charles Bertrand Lewis)

---

* This has been adapted to other fields, such as mining.

Good trade and well paid.

May the weight of our taxes never bend the back of our credit.

Our mints: the only places that make money without advertising.

Though confidence is very fine,
    And makes the future sunny;
I want no confidence in mine,
    I'd rather have the money.

COOKING

May we always have more occasion for the cook than for the doctor.

God sends meat, the devil sends cooks.
—CHARLES VI

DENTISTRY

To the Dentist:
Who, East, West, North, and South,
Always lives from hand to mouth.

'Twould make a suffering mortal grin,
    And laugh away dull care,
If he could see his dentist in
    Another dentist's chair.

FIREFIGHTING

Good attachment, free plugs, full pumps, and fair play to all true firemen.

May he never be *toasted* save by the glass of his friends.

Our Fire Department—the army that draws water instead of blood, and thanks instead of tears.

GARDENING

From the earth we were formed,
    To the earth we return . . .
And in between we garden.
—NELSON EDDY, contributor to *A Gentleman's Guide to Toasting*

Great God of little things
Look upon my labors
Make my little garden
A little better than my neighbor's!

May the weeds wilt before you; may the vegetables rise up to feed you;
and may the bugs stay always on the other side of the fence.
—KATHRYN E. MASON, quoted as an "old hoer's prayer" in the *American Way* magazine, December 1982

GENERAL

An honest lawyer, a pious divine, and a skillful physician.
May the work that you have be the play that you love!
—E. GERBERDING

Oh let us love our occupations,
Bless the squire and his relations,
Live upon our daily rations,
And always know our proper stations.
—CHARLES DICKENS, *The Chimes*

LAW

A bad compromise beats a good lawsuit.

A bumper of good liquor
Will end a contest quicker
Than justice, judge, or vicar;
So fill a cheerful glass,
And let good humor pass.
—RICHARD BRINSLEY SHERIDAN, *The Duenna*, Act II

A countryman between two lawyers is like a fish between two cats.
—BENJAMIN FRANKLIN

And do as adversaries do in law—
Strive mightily, but eat and drink as friends.
—WILLIAM SHAKESPEARE, *The Taming of the Shrew*, Act I

Fond of doctors, little health;
Fond of lawyers, little wealth.

Here's a toast to a man of great trials and many convictions.

Justice while she winks at crimes,
Stumbles on innocence sometimes.
—SAMUEL BUTLER

Litigious terms, fat contentions, and flowing fees.
—JOHN MILTON

May the depths of our potations never cause us to let judgment go by default.

May the judgments of our Benches never be biased.

May we always lie upon our left sides, since the law will not permit us to sleep on our rights.

The glorious uncertainty of the law.
—THOMAS WILBRAHAM

The law: It has honored us; may we honor it.
—DANIEL WEBSTER

The lawyer—a learned gentleman, who rescues your estate from your enemies, and keeps it himself.

To Lawyers: You cannot live without the lawyers, and certainly you cannot die without them.
—Joseph H. Choate

"Virtue in the middle," said the Devil, as he seated himself between two lawyers.*

When a festive occasion our spirit unbends
We should never forget the profession's best friends.
So we'll pass round the wine
And a light bumper fill
To the jolly testator who makes his own will.

Who lied to me about his case,
And said we'd have an easy race,
And did it all with solemn face?
    My client.

Who taught me first to litigate,
My neighbor and my brother hate,
And my own rights overrate?
    My lawyer.

MEDICINE

And Nathan, being sick, trusted not in the lord, but sent for a physician—and Nathan was gathered unto his fathers.
—Old Testament

The doctors are our friends, let's please them well,
For though they kill but slow they are certain.
—Francis Beaumont and John Fletcher

---

* This toast sometimes ends with the word "editors."

To mankind we drink:—'tis a pleasant task:
Heaven bless it and multiply its wealth;
But it is a little too much to ask
That we should drink to its health.

Unto our doctors let us drink,
    Who cure our chills and ills,
No matter what we really think
    About their pills and bills.
—Philip McAllister

When Judgment Day arrives and all
The doctors answer for their sins,
Oh think of what they'll get who bring
The howling triplets and the twins.

MINING

May all your labors be in vein.
—Yorkshire miner's toast

NOVICE

Here's to learning the ropes without coming unraveled.

POLICE

Here's to the policeman who passes our way.
Here's to the mailman who calls every day.
Here's to the babies who continually say:
"Mom, which is my daddy—the blue or the gray?"

POLITICS

Here's to the honest politician—a man who when bought stays
bought.

THE PRESS

A health to the slaves of the ink-pot,
    Who, careless of fortune or fame,
Will give their best years (missing brilliant careers)
    And all for the love of the game!
—JAMES P. HAVERSON

Here's to the bulldog! Here's to the best of the past!
—JERRY GRAY, weekend national editor toasting the remaining staff when
    the *New York Times* moved to a new building in 2007. A bulldog is the
    first edition of a paper.

Here's to the press—the "tongue" of the country; may it never be cut
out.

The liberty of the press and success to its defenders.

The Newspaper—may it fight like an army in the defense of right
with strong columns and good leaders.

The Press of Our Country: The engine of our liberty, the terror of
tyrants, and the schoolmaster of the whole world.

The Press: the great bulwark of our liberties, and may it ever remain
unshackled.
—American, eighteenth century

The Press: the great corrector of abuses, the shield of the oppressed,
and the terror of the oppressor.

We editors may dig and toil
    Till our fingertips are sore,
But some poor fish is sure to say,
"I've heard that joke before."

PRINTING

The master of all trades: he beats the farmer with his fast "hoe," the carpenter with his "rule," and the mason in "setting up his columns"; he surpasses the lawyer and the doctor in attending to the "cases," and beats the person in the management of the devil.

You can always tell a barber
    By the way he parts his hair;
You can always tell a dentist
    When you're in the dentist's chair;
And even a musician—
    You can tell him by his touch;
You can always tell a printer,
    But you cannot tell him much.

A PROMOTION

Here's to becoming top banana without losing touch with the bunch.

—BILL COPELAND in the *Sarasota Journal*

PSYCHIATRY

Here's to my psychiatrist. He finds you cracked and leaves you broke.

SALES

Let's drink to my sales manager's health so I'll have a reason to put these on my expense account.

—Cartoon caption in *Esquire*, April 1955

Never sell a salesman short.

SECURITIES

He keeps us poor all our lives so we can die rich.

WAITERING

We drink your health, O Waiter!
    And may you be preserved
From old age, gout, or sudden death!—
    At least till supper's served.
—OLIVER HERFORD and JOHN CECIL CLAY, *Happy Days*

WRITING

Authors are judged by strange, capricious rules. The great ones are thought mad, the small ones fools.

To an American author: Though a true democrat, may you always keep within touch of royalty!

To the writer's very good health. May he live to be as old as his jokes!

Writing is a dog's life, but the only life worth living.
—GUSTAVE FLAUBERT

SEE ALSO: *Special People*

PROHIBITION

A dry heaven, and a wet hell;
So it is prohibitors tell;
But who would to a desert go,
When it's nice and wet and soggy
    Down below?

Forty miles from whiskey,
    And sixty miles from gin,
I'm leaving this damn country,
    For to live a life of sin.

Four and twenty Yankees,
    feeling very dry,
Went across the border
    to get a drink of rye.

When the rye was opened,
    the Yanks began to sing,
"God bless America,
    but God save the King!"
—Song/toast popular in Canada during prohibition

God bless America and damn prohibition.

Here's to Carry Nation,
Of antidrink renown,
Who, though against libation,
Hit ev'ry bar in town!

Here's to prohibition: May it continue to reduce the number of men
who think they can sing.

Here's to prohibition,
The devil take it!
They've stolen our wine,
So now we make it.

Here's to the "noble experiment"'s ignoble death!

Liberty—may it ever be enjoyed by Americans without prohibition.

May you get through the passport office without detention, through
Europe with dissention, and through customs without detection.

Mother makes brandy from cherries;
Pop distills whiskey and gin;
Sister sells wine from the grapes on our vine
Good grief how the money rolls in.

Ship me somewhere east of Suez,
　　where the best is like the worst,
Where there aren't no ten commandments an' a man
　　can raise a thirst.
　—RUDYARD KIPLING, used as prohibition lament

Thirsty days hath September,
April, June, and November;
All the rest are thirsty too
Except for him who hath home brew.

To my bootlegger: Here's hoping he never has to drink any
of his own.

When Christ turned water into wine
There were no drys to scold and whine;
Today prohibitors would rail
And send the Son of God to jail.

When men were free as a matter of course,
　　Millions of dollars in revenue came;
While now millions go, a law to enforce,
　　And all but the bootleggers lose at the game.

Wise guys
　　Buy supplies;
Dry guys
　　Likewise.

SEE ALSO: *Historic; Temperance*

QUOTES (WHICH ARE NOT EXACTLY TOASTS BUT WHICH BELONG IN A BOOK LIKE THIS)

Do not worry; eat three square meals a day; say your prayers; be courteous to your creditors; keep your digestion good; exercise; go slow, and easy. Maybe there are other things that your special case requires to make you happy, but, my friend, these I reckon will give you a good lift.
—Abraham Lincoln

House Rules. The bar of the National Press Club in Washington, D.C., once displayed a quotation from the Holy Rule of St. Benedict, a directive for conduct issued by the early monastic order:

> If any pilgrim monk come from distant parts, with wish as a guest to dwell in the monastery, and will be content with the customs which he finds in the place, and do not perchance by his lavishness disturb the monastery, but is simply content with what he finds, he shall be received for as long a time as he desires. If, indeed, he find fault with anything, or expose it, reasonably, and with the humility of charity, the Abbot shall discuss it prudently, lest perchance God had sent him for this very thing. But, if he have been found gossipy and contumacious in the time of his sojourn as guest, it shall be said to him, honestly, that he must depart. If he does not go, let two stout monks, in the name of God, explain the matter to him.

I feel no pain dear mother now,
But Oh I am so dry.
Oh take me to a brewery
And leave me there to die.
—Anonymous

I kissed my first woman and smoked my first cigarette on the same day. I have never had time for tobacco since.
—Arturo Toscanini

I really don't deserve this. But I have arthritis and don't deserve that either.
—Jack Benny on accepting an award

In the sixteenth century when there were no Water Boards, water was really dangerous to drink; everybody in England drank ale, beer and wine. England's population then was less than the population of London to-day, and the quota of great statesmen, soldiers, sailors, philosophers, poets and dramatists reared on beer and wine in those days compares favourably with the greatness reached in our own sober times.
—A. L. Simmons, *Daily Telegraph*, April 1931

Leave the flurry
To the masses;
Take your time
And shine your glasses.
—Old Shaker verse

Mankind are earthen jugs with spirits in them.
—Nathaniel Hawthorne

My temples throb, my pulses boil,
    I'm sick of Song and Ode and Ballad—
So Thyrsis, take the midnight oil,
    And pour it on a lobster salad.
—Thomas Hood, "To Minerva"

Saw a wedding in the church and strange to see what delight we married people have to see these poor fools decoyed into our condition.
—Samuel Pepys, diary entry, December 25, 1665

The best audience is one that is intelligent, well educated—and a little drunk.
—Vice President Alben W. Barkley

There must be more beer, cheaper beer, better beer! People who do not drink beer do not realize that beer is as important to the working classes as bread . . . Men who find they cannot get beer tend to develop a taste for less innocent liquors. Good ale and good beer are drinks of temperate men, and it must be confessed that England has bred a race of mighty fighting men on her national brew. Good beer is the basis of true temperance.
—*Daily Express*, January 25, 1919

This North American has been a inmate of my 'ouse ove two weeks, yit he hasn't made no attempts to scalp any member of my family. He hasn't broke no cups or sassers, or furniture of any kind. (Hear, hear.) I find I can trust him with lited candles. He eats his vittles with a knife and a fork. People of this kind should be encurridged. I purpose 'is 'elth. (Loud 'plaws.)
—To Artemus Ward, from *Punch*, 1866

When Woodrow proposed to me, I was so surprised I nearly fell out of bed.
—Attributed to the second Mrs. Woodrow Wilson

SEE ALSO: *Secrets*

REUNIONS

Here's a health in homely rhyme
To our oldest classmate, Father Time;
May our last survivor live to be
As bold and wise and as thorough as he!
—OLIVER WENDELL HOLMES

Here's to all of us!
For there's so much good in the worst of us
    And so much bad in the best of us,
That it hardly behooves any of us,
    To talk about the rest of us.

Some among many gather again,
A glass to their happiness; friendship,
Amen . . .
The Survivors.
—JAMES MONROE MCLEAN, *The Book of Wine*

Then fill the cup, fill high! fill high!
    Let joy our goblets crown,
We'll bung Misfortune's scowling eye,
    And knock Foreboding down.
—JAMES RUSSELL LOWELL, from "To the Class of '38"

To friends: As long as we are able
To lift our glasses from the table.

To the good old days . . . we weren't so good, 'cause we weren't so old!

SEE ALSO: *Colleges and Universities; Friendship; Parting; Past, Present, and Future*

REVELRY

A very merry, dancing, drinking,
Laughing, quaffing, and unthinking time.
—JOHN DRYDEN

Alcohol—a liquid good for preserving almost anything except secrets.
—GIDEON WORDZ

And the night shall be filled with music,
     And the cares that infest the day
Shall fold their tents like the Arabs,
     And as silently steal away.
—Henry Wadsworth Longfellow

But, fill me with the old familiar juice,
Methinks I might recover bye and bye.
—Omar Khayyám

Care to our coffin adds a nail, no doubt,
And every grain, so merry, draws one out.
—John Wolcott

Drink to the girls and drink to their mothers,
Drink to their fathers and to their brothers;
Toast their dear healths as long as you're able,
And dream of their charms while under the table.

Drinking will make a man quaff,
Quaffing will make a man sing,
Singing will make a man laugh,
And laughing long life doth bring.
—Thomas D'Urfey

Enough you know when this is said,
That, one and all—they died in bed!
—Charles Henry Webb, *Dum Vivimus Vigilamus*

Fill up the bowl, upon my soul,
     Your trouble you'll forget, sir;
If it takes more, fill twenty more,
     Till you have drowned regret, sir.

Fill up the goblet and reach me some,
Drinking makes wise, but dry feasting makes glum.
—Asian

Here is a riddle most abstruse:
    Cans't read the answer right?
Why is it that my tongue grows loose
    Only when I grow tight?

Here, waiter, more wine, let me sit while I'm able,
Till all my companions sink under the table.
—OLIVER GOLDSMITH

Here's pleasure as you like it.

Here's to a guy who is never blue,
Here's to a buddy who is ever true,
Here's to a pal, no matter what the load,
Who never declines one for the road.

Here's to a long life and a merry one,
A quick death and an easy one,
A pretty girl and a true one,
A cold bottle and another one.

I'm tired of drinking toasts
For each small glass of gin.
Let's toss out all the hooey
And toss the liquor in.

In for a high old frolic,
Chiefly alcoholic.

Laugh at all things,
Great and small things,
Sick and well, at sea or shore;
While we are quaffing,
Let's have laughing.
Who the devil cares for more?
—LORD BYRON

Let us have wine and women, mirth and laughter,
Sermons and soda water the day after.
—LORD BYRON

Let us sip and let it slip
    And go which way it will-a
Let us trip and let us ship
    And let us drink our fill-a.

Let's live in haste; use pleasures while we may:
Could life return, 'twould never lose a day.
—ROBERT HERRICK

Raise your glasses, lift them high,
Drink to health dear toasters;
But when you set them down again,
Can't you hit our coasters?
—D. S. HALACY JR., *1000 Jokes*, May–July 1955, "The Ringleavers"

Said Aristotle unto Plato,
    "Have another sweet potato?"
Said Plato unto Aristotle,
    "Thank you, I prefer the bottle."
—OWEN WISTER

The more I drink, the better I sing.

They tell me my love would in time have been cloy'd,
And that Beauty's insipid when once 'tis enjoyed;
But in wine I both time and enjoyment defy,
For the longer I drink the more thirsty am I.

Too much work, and no vacation,
Deserves at least a small libation.
So hail! my friends, and raise your glasses;
Work's the curse of the drinking classes.

Toss the pot, toss the pot; let us be merry,
And drink till our cheeks be red as a cherry.
—Anonymous, circa 1600

Turn out more ale, turn up the light;
I will not go to bed tonight.
Of all the foes that man should dread
The first I have had both old and young,
And ale we drank and songs we sung.

What would you like to drink to?
To about three in the morning.

Who loves not women, wine, and song,
Remains a fool his whole life long.
—Johann Heinrich Voss

You're a purty man!—you air!
With a pair o' eyes like two fried eggs
An' a nose like a Bartlutt Pear!

SEE ALSO: *Beer and Ale; Champagne; Libations; Lust; Mornings After; Spirits (Ardent); Ultimate Toasts; Wine*

ST. PATRICK'S DAY

May the Irish hills caress you.
May her lakes and rivers bless you.
May the luck of the Irish enfold you.
May the blessings of St. Patrick behold you.

May the leprechauns be near you to spread luck along your way,
and may all the Irish angels smile upon you on St. Pat's Day.

On St. Patrick's Day, you should spend time with saints and scholars, so of course, you know, I have two more stops I have to make.
—RONALD REAGAN, at a St. Patrick's Day luncheon on Capitol Hill, 1988

St. Patrick was a gentleman,
    Who, through strategy and stealth,
Drove all the snakes from Ireland—
    Here's a bumper to his health.
But not too many bumpers,
    Lest we lose ourselves, and then
Forget the good St. Patrick,
    And see the snakes again.

Success attend St. Patrick's fist,
    For he's a saint so clever;
Oh! he give the snakes and toads a twist,
    He banished them forever.

The anniversary of St. Patrick's Day—and may the shamrock be green forever.

SEE ALSO: *Irish*

SCOTCH

A guid New Year to yin and a'
    And mony may you see,
And may the mouse ne'er run out o'
    Your girnel wi' a tear in its 'e.

Blythe may we a' be,
I'll may we never see!

Here's grand luck, an' muckle fat weans [big, fat children]!

Here's health ta the seeck, an' stilts ta the lame;
Claise ta the back, an' brose ta the wame [gruel to the belly]!

Here's tae auld Scotland, the land o' our birth,
Wi' its hulls where stormy winds whistle.
Ye can sit for a month on the shamrock an' the rose,
But ye canna sit land on the thistle!

Here's tae us! Wha's like us?
      Da' few and they're deed.
[Here's to us! Who's like us?
      Damn few and they're dead.]

Here's to them that lo'es us, or lends us a lift.

May the best ye've ever seen
Be the worst ye'll ever see.

May the mouse ne'er leave our meal pock wi' the tear in its ee.

May the winds o' adversity ne'er blaw open our door.

May your life
Be like good Scotch
Smooth and clear
And like good Scotch
May it improve
With every passing year.

O, wad, some pow'r the giftie gie us
To see oursels as others see us!
It wad frae money a blunder free us.
—Robert Burns

The deil rock them in the creel that does na' wish us a' weel.

Then let us toast John Barleycorn,
    Each man a glass in hand;
And may his great posterity
    Ne'er fail in old Scotland!

Up wi' yer glesses, an' deil tak the hindmaist!

SEE ALSO: *New Year's; Ultimate Toasts*

SECRETS

Here's a collection of ancestral information that has been lost to the modern world.

EIGHT CONDITIONS OF OVERINDULGENCE

The first is Ape drunke, and he leapes, and sings, and hollowes, daunceth for the heavens: the second is Lion drunke, and he flings the pots about the house, calls his Hostesse whore, breakes the glasse windowes with his dagger, and is apt to quarrell with any man that speaks to him. The third is Swine drunke, heavy, lumpish and sleepy. The fourth is Sheepe drunk, wise in his own conceit, when he cannot bring forth a right word. The fifth is Mawdlin drunk, when a fellow weep for kindness in the middle of his ale, and kiss you saying "By God Captain I love you." The sixth is Martin drunke, when a man is drunke and drinks himself sober ere he stir. The seventh is Goat drunk—with his mind on naught but lechery. The eight is Foxe drunke, when he is craftie drunk, as many of the Dutch men be, will never bargain but when they ave drunk.
—From *Pierce Penniless*, by Thomas Nashe, 1592

SIX WAYS TO PREVENT INTOXICATION

1. Take white cabbage's, and four pomegranate's juices, two ounces of each, with one of vinegar. Boil all together for some time to the consistence of a syrup. Take one ounce of this before you are going to drink, and drink afterwards as much, and as long, as you please.

2. Eat five or six bitter almonds fasting; this will have the same effect.

3. It is affirmed that if you eat mutton or goat's lungs roasted; cabbage, or any feed; or wormwood, it will absolutely prevent the bad effects which result from the excess of drinking.

4. You may undoubtedly prevent the accidents resulting from hard drinking, if before dinner you eat, in salad, four or five tops of raw cabbages.

5. Take some swallows' beaks, and burn them in a crucible. When perfectly calcined crush them on a stone, and put some of that powder in a glass of wine, and drink it. Whatever wine you may drink to excess afterwards, it will have no effect upon you. The whole body of the swallow, prepared in the same manner, will have the same effect.

6. Pound in a mortar the leaves of a peach-tree, and squeeze the juice of them in a basin. Then, fasting, drink a full glass of that liquor, and take whatever excess of wine you will on that day, you will not be intoxicated.
—From *Valuable Secrets Concerning Arts and Trades*, 1795

THREE MONGOL SECRETS FOR TIPPLING
1. Never force yourself to eat, and never get angry, when you are under the influence of drink or you will break out in boils. Washing the face in cold water has the same effect.

2. Don't ride or jump about, or exert yourself in any way when drunk or you will injure your bones and sinews and undermine your strength.

3. If you see in your wine the reflection of a person not in your range of vision, don't drink it.
—From *The Imperial Cookery Book of the Mongol Dynasty*

HOW TO REFORM THOSE WHO DRINK
TOO MUCH WINE

Put in a sufficient quantity of wine three or four large eels, which leave there till quite dead. Give that wine to drink to the person you want to reform, and he or she will be so much disgusted of wine, that tho' they formerly made much use of it, they will now have quite an aversion to it.

—From *Valuable Secrets Concerning Arts and Trades*, 1795

TO REFRESH A LARGE NUMBER OF PEOPLE

In 1694 Admiral Edward Russell, commanding the Mediterranean fleet, gave a grand entertainment at Alicant. The tables were laid under the shade of orange trees in four garden walks meeting at a common centre, where there stood a handsome marble fountain. This fountain was converted for the occasion into a gigantic punch-bowl. Four hogsheads of brandy, one pipe of Malaga wine, twenty gallons of lime-juice, twenty-five hundred lemons, thirteen hundred-weight of fine white sugar, five pounds' weight of grated nutmegs, three hundred toasted biscuits, and eight hogsheads of water, formed the ingredients of this monster potation. An elegant canopy placed over the potent liquor prevented waste by evaporation or dilution by rain. To crown this titanic effort, a small boy was placed in a boat expressly built for the purpose, to row round the fountain and assist in landing the punch into the cups of the six thousand persons who were invited to partake of it.

—From *Inns, Ales, and Drinking Customs of Old England*,
   by Frederick W. Hackwood, 1909

TO PROPERLY TOAST ANOTHER

He that beginnes the health hath prescribed orders; first uncovering his head he takes a full cup in his hand, and settling his countenance with a grave aspect, he crave an audience; silence being once obtained, he begins to breathe out the name peradventure of some honourable personage, that was worthy of a better regard than to have his name polluted at so unfitting a time, amongst a company of drunkards, but his health is drunk to, and he that pledges must likewise off with his cap, kisse his fingers, and bow himself in sign of reverent acceptance. When the leader sees his follower thus prepared, he sups up his breath, turns the bottom of his cup upward, and in ostentation of his dexteritie gives the cup a phillip to make it cry twange, and thus the first scene is acted.

—From *The Irish Hubbub; or, The English Hue and Crie*,
   by Barnabe Rich, 1617

DRINK FORMULA CALLING FOR ONE COW ALE
SYLLABUB

Place in a large bowl a quart of strong ale or beer, grate into it a little nutmeg, and sweeten it with sugar. Milk the cow rapidly into the bowl, forcing the milk as strongly as possible into the ale, and against the sides of the vessel, to raise a good froth. Let it stand for an hour and it will then be fit for use. Cider may be used instead of ale, and the sugar should be proportioned to the taste of the drinker.

—Eighteenth-century England

RECIPE FOR AN AFTER-DINNER SPEECH

Three long breaths.
Compliment to the audience.
Funny story.
Outline of what speaker is *not* going to say.
Points that he will touch on later.
Two Bartlett's Familiar Quotations.
Outline of what speaker *is* going to say.
Points that he has not time to touch on now.
Reference to what he said first.
Funny story.
Compliment to the audience.
Ditto to our City, State, and Country.
Applause.
N.B. For an oration, use same formula, repeating each sentence three times in slightly different words.

—MARY ELEANOR ROBERTS

A SELECTED GLOSSARY OF TOAST AND TIPPLE

Herewith some special terms for special occasions.

ABSINTHE Makes the heart grow fonder.

ALL NATIONS A vile drink composed of the dregs of various casks, to which strong beer was sometimes added.

BEVERAGE Derives from the word *bever*, which is a drink taken between meals. Eton College, for instance, once had bever days, when extra beer was served to the students.

BINDER The last drink of the evening.

BREWPUB A bar/restaurant where beer is brewed on the premises. John Mitchell pioneered America's first brewpub in 1982.

BRIDAL We all know what this means, but what is interesting is that it comes from an old English custom of the "bride-ale," by which the bride was given the proceeds from the sale of ale at her wedding.

BRIMMER A glass so full that the liquid touches the brim. Although the liquid has climbed to the brim, there is a slight depression or hollow in the center of the surface. A *bumper* (see below) is a brimmer to which extra drops have been added to fill the hollow to a bump. The difference between a brimmer and a bumper can be demonstrated by floating a cork fragment on the surface. The cork will float to the edge of a brimmer, while it will sit in the middle of a bumper.

BUMPER A glass filled to the extreme. Bumpers are often used in toasting and sometimes taken in one draft. There are two explanations for the term: (1) It comes from the French *au ban pe*, or "good father," and is attributed to the medieval custom of dedicating the first cup of wine to the pope; (2) it comes from a glass filled so high that the liquid "bumps" up in the middle, higher in the center than at the brim. (See *brimmer*, above.)

DROP There are 60 drops in a teaspoon; 120 in a dessertspoon; 240 in a tablespoon; 480 in an ounce; 960 in a wineglass; 1,920 in a teacup; 3,840 in a breakfast cup or tumbler; 7,680 in a pint; 15,360 in a quart; 61,440 in a gallon; 2,935,360 in a barrel; 3,870,720 in a hogshead. Its equivalent weight is .9493 grams. A drop is equal to a minim. (From *The Banquet Book*, by Cuyler Reynolds, 1902)

FLAP-DRAGON An Elizabethan drink with a flammable surface, ignited for hard drinkers to quaff in one fast gulp. Drinking these was called "flap-dragoning," a custom Shakespeare references in several of his works.

FLIGHT A sampling of wine, beer, Scotch, or another beverage offered for a flat price. A way of getting a taste of several varieties.

FOB A brewer's term for beer froth.

HOBNOB The quaint custom of sitting around the "hob," or projecting corner of a fireplace, and drinking.

LONGNECK A beer bottle with a long neck. There is a certain bravado associated with carrying one around a bar, especially a Lone Star longneck in Texas.

LOVING CUP A massive common cup that's passed from hand to hand as a token of peace. It usually has three handles. Today these are largely ornamental and used as trophies. A number of stories purport to state the origin of the loving cup. One that makes as much sense as the rest and is the most interesting explanation is this: King Henry V was out riding, became thirsty, and stopped at the door of a country inn for a cup of wine. The barmaid handed it to him by its single handle, forcing him to take it in both hands, thereby soiling his gloves. The king made up his mind that this would not happen again, so he had a cup made with two handles, which he then had sent to the inn for his private use. When he next happened on the inn, he again ordered a cup of wine. The same barmaid served him, this time grasping the cup by its two handles. The problem was solved when he ordered that a three-handled cup be made.

MOCKTAIL A nonalcoholic mixed drink created with the flair associated with an alcoholic mixed drink. These are often named after celebrities, a tradition that may have started with the classic "Shirley Temple" drink, named after the child actress of the early twentieth century. Other popular mocktails are the Arnold Palmer and the more current Tiger Woods.

THE ARNOLD PALMER

Ingredients
3 ounces lemonade
3 ounces iced tea

Preparation
Pour the lemonade and iced tea into a Tom Collins glass filled with ice. Stir well.

THE TIGER WOODS

Ingredients
3 ounces brewed green tea
1 ounce kalamansi lime puree
1 teaspoon honey
Club soda

Preparation
Stir together the green tea, lime puree, and honey. Pour the mixture into an ice-filled highball glass and top with club soda. (From the April 2009 *Spirit*, Southwest Airlines' magazine)

NEBUCHADNEZZAR Until 1986 the largest size of champagne bottle, capable of holding enough to fill 104 glasses. Its counterparts are, in decreasing size, the 83-glass *Balthazar*, 62-glass *Salmanazar*, 41-glass *Methusela*, 31-glass *Rehoboam*, 21-glass *Jeroboam*, and 10-glass *Magnum*. A standard bottle holds a mere 5 glasses. (See also *Salomon*.)

NIP One sixth of a quartern (a five-ounce measure).

NOGGIN An old ale measure for a quarter pint. The word appears in old drinking songs such as one with this line:

Before we think of jogging,
Let's take a cheerful noggin.

NO HEEL TAPS An old drinking injunction meaning to finish your glass—leave no dregs.

PIGGIN A drinking vessel made from a pig's skin. It is one of a number of leather vessels of yore including the bombard, gaspin, and blackjack. Other bygone vessels include the crinze (earthenware), the mazer (wood), and the quaich (silver or china). In former times, it seems, just about anything might end up being used as a cup. A writer of 1635 tells of all the predictable materials for drinking vessels, including old boots, and then adds, "We have, besides, cups made out of homes of beasts, of cockernuts, of goords, of the eggs of ostriches; others made of the shells of diverse fishes, brought from the Indies and other places, and shining like mother-of-pearle."

PITCHER Pouring vessel originally made of leather and so called because it was lined with pitch to make it waterproof.

PONY A glass holding about a mouthful of spirits.

PUNCH Although used less specifically today, the word originally referred to a drink of five ingredients: liquor, water, lemon, sugar, and spice.

PUNCHEON A wine measure equal to 2 tierces, or 84 gallons, or 336 quarts, or 672 pints.

ROAST Different than a toast, viz.,

When T stands for tender
And R stands for rough
You've the difference twixt a
Toast and a Roast.
—STANLICUS

SALOMON As of 1986 the largest champagne bottle ever produced, capable of containing the equivalent of 24 750-milliliter bottles. Seven of them were mouth-blown in France on the occasion of the centennial of the Statue of Liberty.

SHOOTER A straight shot meant to be consumed in one gulp. Also, a house drink that is usually sweet and easy to consume quickly; these are common at beach bars and often feature a fruit liqueur, such as De Kuyper peach schnapps, Southern Comfort, or tequila.

SPLASH A small amount of water or soda, as in "bourbon with a splash."

STIRRUP CUP One for the road. The name for the drink given to a departing guest whose feet were already in the stirrups.

TEETOTALER The term comes from a pledge of an 1830s Michigan temperance society. Members were offered two pledges: one calling for moderate drinking, the other calling for total abstinence. On the membership rolls, the moderates were identified as "O.P.," for "Old Pledge," and those who swore off drinking entirely were identified as "T-Total." They were soon called "teetotalers."

TOAST The only thing that can be eaten or drunk.

TODDY A sweet drink of whiskey, water, and sugar that is often warmed. *Toddy* is a corruption of *tārī*, the Hindu name for a sweet palm juice.

TUMBLER A common drinking glass that was originally a drinking horn unevenly weighted with lead at the bottom. This was done to encourage the drinker to drain the contents in one draft, as the vessel was so weighted that it could not be put down without tumbling over. The tumbler is believed to be of Saxon origin.

WATER Liquid of which ice is made.

WET YOUR WHISTLE To drink. The term reputedly comes from an old Scottish custom of awarding a silver whistle to the winner of a drinking contest. These contests were decided when only one participant was left standing and able to blow the whistle. One such contest was won by a Scotch nobleman who bested a boastful Dane after several days and nights of drinking. Robert Burns wrote of the memorable contest:

I sing of a Whistle, a Whistle of worth;
I sing of a Whistle, the pride of the North
Was brought to the Court of our good Scottish King,
And long with this Whistle all Scotland shall ring.

WOOD-FINISHED Scotch or bourbon embellished by being stored in casks originally used for port, sherry, and other products

SEE ALSO: *Ultimate Toasts*

SELF AND SELVES

Here's health to my soul and health to my heart,
Where this is going, there's gone many a quart.
Through my teeth and round my gums;
Look out, belly, here it comes!

Here's to ourselves
And wishing all
The wish they wish themselves!

Here's to the health of those we love best—
Our noble selves—God bless us;
None better and many a damn sight worse.
Drink to-day, and drown all sorrow;
You shall, perhaps, not do it to-morrow.
—Francis Beaumont and John Fletcher

Here's to you,
     And here's to me;
But as you're not here,
     Here's two to me.

I was the toast of two continents: Greenland and Australia.
—Dorothy Parker

Life is a banquet and most poor sons-of-bitches are starving to
death.
—Patrick Dennis, *Auntie Mame*

Our noble selves—may we never be less.

Our noble selves—why not toast ourselves, and praise ourselves;
since we have the best means of knowing all the good in ourselves.

Well! Here's luck, great luck,
Such luck as never was known;
May the winner's pockets bulge with coin,
And these pockets be—my own.

SHAKESPEAREAN

A flock of blessings light upon thy back.
—*Romeo and Juliet*, Act III

A health, gentlemen,
Let it go round.
—*Henry VIII*, Act I

Come, come, good wine is a good familiar creature, if it be well used;
exclaim no more against it.
—*Othello*, Act II

Drink down all unkindness.
—*The Merry Wives of Windsor*, Act I

Fair thought and happy hours attend on you.
—*The Merchant of Venice*, Act III

Fill the cup and let it come,
I'll pledge you a mile to the bottom.
—*Henry IV, Part II*, Act III

Frame your mind to mirth and merriment,
Which bars a thousand harms and lengthens life.
—*The Taming of the Shrew*, Act II

God's benison go with you; and with those
That would make good of bad, and
friends of foes.
—*Macbeth*, Act II

I wish all good befortune you!
—*The Two Gentlemen of Verona*, Act IV

I wish you all the joy you can wish.
—*The Merchant of Venice*, Act III

Let's drink together friendly, and embrace.
—*Henry IV, Part II*, Act IV

Love sought is good, but given unsought is better.
—*Twelfth Night*, Act III

Speak no more of her. Give me a bowl of wine:
In this I bury all unkindness.
—*Julius Caesar*, Act IV

The best of happiness, honor, and fortunes keep with you.
—*Timon of Athens*, Act I

They do not love that do not show their love.
—*The Two Gentlemen of Verona*, Act I

To make the coming hour o'erflow and joy,
And pleasure drown the brim.
—*All's Well That Ends Well*, Act II

You have deserved his commendation, true applause and love.
—*As You Like It*, Act I

SKOALING

Scandinavian toasting hinges for the most part on one word, *skål*, or in its an-glicized version, *skoal*. It is a particular kind of toasting with its own protocol. For starters, one is supposed to engage the eyes of the person toasted and keep the gaze locked until the act is completed and the glass returned to a point be-low the neck. One must also know when to skoal. The Swedish Information Service provides these guidelines for anyone planning a formal Swedish dinner or expecting an invitation to Stockholm to pick up his or her Nobel Prize:

Host usually starts by a toast of welcome.
Host then usually drinks with the ladies, one at a time.
Hostess usually begins by drinking with the gentlemen, one at a time.
Guests *do not* toast host or hostess.

Gentlemen toast the ladies, beginning with lady on right, then on left.
Ladies usually do not return the toast.
Gentlemen toast each other.
The older or more prominent person always takes the initiative;
    the younger returns the toast before the end of dinner.
Some younger ladies return older ladies' toasts, some don't.
You usually answer a toast in the same wine.

SPECIAL OCCASIONS

AFTER A QUARREL
Here's looking at you, though heaven knows it's an effort.

APRIL 15
We know it is true that we're wicked,
    That our criminal laws are lax;
But here's to punishment for the man
    Who invented our income tax.

BEFORE AN EXAM

If we must suffer, let us suffer nobly.
—VICTOR HUGO

COCKTAIL PARTY

To the cocktail party: where olives are speared and friends stabbed.

CONSCIENCE, MOMENTS OF

Here's to a clear conscience—or a poor memory.

Here's to Conscience. May it waken to hear us toast it and then go to sleep again.

FOUR OF US

Here's to the four of us!
Thank God there's no more of us!

Or

One bottle for four of us!
Thank God there's no more of us!

GRADUATION

A toast to the graduate—in a class by him-herself.

IMPERFECT LOVE

Here's to the man who can bravely say,
"I have loved her all my life—
Since I took her hand on the wedding day
I have only loved my wife!"
Would we not praise him long and well
With the strongest praise that is,
The man who could boldly, firmly tell,
And stick to—a lie like this?

Marriage is a lot like the army: Everyone complains, but you'd be surprised at the large number that reenlist.
—JAMES GARNER, actor

Needles and pins, needles and pins, when a man marries, his trouble begins.

'Tis better to have loved and lost,
Than to marry and be bossed.

You may prate of the virtue of memory,
Of the days and joys that are past,
But here's to a good forgettery,
And a friendship that cannot last!
You may talk of a woman's constancy,
And the love that cannot die,
But here's a health to a woman's coquetry,
And the pleasure of saying "Good-Bye"!
—A written toast left at the Wayside Inn, from Henry Wadsworth
   Longfellow's *Tales of a Wayside Inn*

JULY 4

The Fourth of July—like oysters, it cannot be enjoyed without crackers.

LABOR DAY

May it for all time be cherished by mankind, may its observance ever be the means of driving away the frowns and shadows of life and bring ease, comfort, and joy to the home of toil. Its purpose is noble—to educate, to elevate, to establish justice. Long live Labor Day!
—W. W. DODGE, state senator from Burlington, Iowa, author of the law
   creating Labor Day in Iowa

To Peter J. McGuire, Thank You.
—McGuire was the union official who in 1882 proposed that the first
   Monday in September be set aside as a day for labor to celebrate its
   "strength and esprit de corps."

LATE ARRIVAL

Here's to the Clock!
　　Whose hands, we pray heaven,
When we come home at three,
　　Have stopped at eleven!
—OLIVER HERFORD and JOHN CECIL CLAY, *Happy Days*

I crept upstairs, my shoes in hand,
　　Just as the night took wing,
And saw my wife, four steps above,
　　Doing the same damned thing.

Then fill a fair and honest cup, and bear it straight to me;
The goblet hallows all it holds, what'er the liquid be;
And may the cherubs on its face protect me from the sin
That dooms one to those dreadful words,
"My dear, where have you been?"
—OLIVER WENDELL HOLMES

LYING

The lie—an abomination unto the Lord, and a very present help in time of trouble.

NIGHTCAP

In days of old the night-cap
Was worn outside the head:
Let's put ours in the inside,
And then—let's go to bed.
—W. E. P. FRENCH

May you sleep like a log, but not like a sawmill.

ON THE ROAD

Here's to you and here's to me,
Whenever we may roam;
And here's to the health and happiness
Of the ones who are left at home.

ON THE TRAIL

A health to the man on the trail tonight;
may his grub hold out; may his dogs keep their legs;
may his matches never misfire.
—JACK LONDON

OPENING NIGHT

A hit, a very palpable hit.
—WILLIAM SHAKESPEARE, *Hamlet*, Act V

QUIET EVENING

To the homely three: A good book, a bright light, and an easy chair.

RELIGION

To church: The first time one goes he has water thrown on him, the
second time he has rice thrown on him, the third time he has dirt
thrown on him.

RIOTING, TO THE PREVENTION OF

O Bacchus who hath sent us wine,
Give us now, we pray,
Wit with drink.
And thou, Minerva, wisdom send,
That we may abstain from rioting.

RUMORS

Two ears and but a single tongue
     By nature's laws to man belong.
The lesson she would teach is clear,
     Repeat but half of what you hear.

SECOND CHOICE

Here's to you, my dear,
And to the dear that's not here, my dear;
But if the dear that's not here, my dear,
Were here, my dear,
I'd not be drinking to you, my dear.

THREE OF US

I'm as dear to you as he,
He's as dear to me as thee,
You're as dear to him as me,
Here's to "three's good company."

TROUBLE

Here's to ya,
Here's for ya,
I wish to hell
I never saw ya.

A VERY SPECIAL INTERLUDE

Where is the heart that would not give
Years of drowsy days and nights,
One little hour, like this, to live—
Full, to the brim, of life's delights?
—THOMAS MOORE

SPECIAL PEOPLE

THE BACHELOR

Here's to single blessedness!

THE BAD SINGER

Swans sing before they die: 'twere no bad thing
Did certain persons die before they sing.

THE BORE

Again I hear that creaking step—
He's rapping at the door!—
Too well I know that boding sound
That ushers in a bore.

I do not tremble when I meet
The stoutest of my foes,
But heaven defend me from the man
Who comes—but never goes.

Society is now one polished horde,
Formed of two mighty tribes—the bores and bored.

The bore: May he give us a few brilliant flashes of silence.

THE COWBOY

Here's to luck, and hoping God will take a likin' to us!
—Cowboy, Dakota Territory, circa 1880

Up to my lips and over my gums;
Look out guts, here she comes.
—Cowboy toast collected by John Lomax and Alan Lomax for their
  Cowboy Songs and Other Frontier Ballads (1916 edition)

CREDITORS

Here's to our creditors—may they be
Endowed with three virtues:
Faith, hope, and charity!

Here's to the creditor—long may he waive.

FAT PEOPLE

A toast to us, my good, fat friends,
To bless the things we eat;
For it has been full many a year,
Since we have seen our feet.

Yet who would lose a precious pound,
By trading sweets for sours?
It takes mighty girth indeed,
To hold such hearts as ours!
—WALLACE IRWIN, "Fat Man's Toast," 1904

THE FINANCIALLY INDISPOSED

'Tis easy enough to say, "Fill 'em!"
When your bank doesn't say, "Overdrawn."
 But the man worthwhile,
 Is the man who can smile,
When every darned cent is gone.

THE HOBO

To the holidays—all 365 of them.

THE LIAR

May every liar be blessed with a good memory!

MEMBER OF CONGRESS

May the members of Congress, while they are in Washington, never
forget that they are the representatives of the people.

MISERS

Here's to misers—whose abstinence gives us the more to drink.

MOTHERS-IN-LAW

Here's to our dear old mother-in-law,
 With all her freaks and capers,
For were it not for dear old Ma,
 What would become of the "comic papers"?

OMAR KHAYYÁM

Here's to old Omar Khayyám—
 I'm stuck on that beggar, I am!
His women and wine are something divine—
 For his verses I don't care a damn!

RICHARD WAGNER

Here's to you, Richard Wagner,
 With your horns and your bassoons.
What a hit you'd have made in music
 Had you only tackled tunes.

THE SMOKER

It isn't the cough
That carries you off;
It's the coffin
They carry you off in.

THE SPENDER

Lift 'em high and drain 'em dry
To the guy who says "My turn to buy!"

THE TREKKIE

Live long and prosper. (In Vulcan, *Dup dor a'az Mubster.*)

THE USURER

May you take as much interest in Heaven
As I know you have taken on Earth.

THE VIRGIN

Here's to _____,
For her, life held no terrors.
Born a virgin, died a virgin—
No hits, no runs, no errors.

SEE ALSO: *Professional and Occupational*

SPIRITS (ARDENT)

A drop of whiskey
Ain't a bad thing right here!
—BRET HARTE

A toast to the three great American birds:
    May you always have an Eagle in your pocket
    A Turkey on your table,
    And Old Crow in your glass.

Don't die of love; in heaven above
  Or hell, they'll not endure you;
Why look so glum when Doctor Rum
  Is waiting for to cure you?
—OLIVER HERFORD

Gentlemen, I have seen water in all of its majesty, pouring in torrents over great falls, rushing madly through deep gorges, and tossing wildly as waves of the oceans. I have seen it in the frozen stillness of a winter pond, in the flowerlike crystals of snowflakes. I have seen it as the soft morning dew, and as the gentle teardrop in the eye of a beautiful lady. But gentlemen, as a beverage, it is a damn failure!
—Anonymous

Fifteen men on the dead man's chest—
  Yo-ho-ho, and a bottle of rum!
Drink and the devil had done for the rest—
  Yo-ho-ho, and a bottle of rum!
—ROBERT LOUIS STEVENSON, *Treasure Island*

Here is to the Irish, a whiskey with heart,
that's smooth as a leprechaun's touch,
yet as soft in its taste as a mother's embrace
and a gentleness saying as much.

Here's to the man without a shirt to his back,
May he deck himself out with a dickey;
And here's to the man, who of rums finds a lack,
May he fill himself up with gin rickey.

How beautiful the water is!
To me 'tis wondrous sweet—
For bathing purposes and such;
But liquor's better neat.
—MRS. C. O. SMITH

If wine tells truth, and so have said the wise;
It makes me laugh to think how brandy lies.
—Oliver Wendell Holmes

Inspiring bold John Barleycorn!
What dangers thou canst make us scorn!
Wi' tippenny we fear nae evil;
Wi' usquebae [whiskey] we'll face the devil!
—Robert Burns, *Tam o'Shanter*

Keep your head cool and your feet warm,
And a glass of good whiskey will do you no harm.

Let those who will, praise fragrant wine,
That slowly brings on dizziness.
    Good whiskey, clear,
     To me is dear,
For two drinks does the business.

May we never be out of spirits.

No fluoride. No pollution. Just pure gin.
—Chon Day, caption to a cartoon in *Playboy*

On land or at sea
One need not be wary:
A well-made old-fashioned
prevents *beri beri*.

Rum, rum, Jamaica rum,
Who in thy praise is dumb?
The rich, the poor, the gay, the glum,
All call thee good, Jamaica Rum.
—Sir Arthur Sullivan

This cordial julep here
That flames and dances in its crystal bounds.
—John Milton, *Comus*

Well, if it isn't gin,
Was meant to do us in,
The chances are it's lemonade or dates.
—A. P. HERBERT, in John Watney's *Mother's Ruin: A History of Gin*

When the mint is in the liquor and
its fragrance is in the glass,
It breathes a recollection that
can never, never pass.
—CLARENCE OUSLEY, quoted in *The Kentucky Mint Julep*,
    by Colonel Joe Nickell

SEE ALSO: *Libations; Mornings After; Prohibition; Revelry*

SPORTS AND GAMES

It would appear that people who write good toasts tend to fish and play poker rather than, say, hunt and play tennis. As the following toasts seem to illustrate, the great toasters have gotten their exercise from hoisting glasses.

A little whiskey now and then
Is relished by the best of men;
It surely drives away dull care,
And makes ace high look like two pair.

Camp life is just one canned thing after another.
—Toast to camping

Gentlemen, the Queen!
She gazed at us serene,
She filled his flush,
Amidst the hush—
And gathered in the green.

Not the laurel—but the race,
Not the quarry—but the chase;
Not the dice—but the play
May I, Lord, enjoy always!

Poker—like a glass of beer, you draw to fill.

The hand that rocks the cradle
    Is the hand that rules the earth.
But the hand that holds four aces—
    Bet on it for all you're worth!

There was a man in our town,
    And he was wondrous wise.
He jumped into a tournament
    And came out with a prize.
And when he saw the cup he'd won,
    With all his might and main,
He jumped into ten entry lists
    But never won again.

They have carried the American name to the uttermost parts of the
earth—and covered it with glory every time. That is a service to
sentiment; but they did the general world a large practical service,
also—a service to the great science of geography . . . Why, when
those boys started out you couldn't see the equator at all; you could
walk right over it and never know it was there . . . But that is all
fixed now . . . And so I drink long life to the boys who ploughed a
new equator round the globe stealing bases on their bellies!
—MARK TWAIN, to the members of the returning Spalding Baseball Tour
    of the World, 1889

SEE ALSO: *Fishing*

STATES

CALIFORNIA

In the fold of the grape let's pledge her,
Land favored by luck and fate,
California must be heaven,
For she owns the golden gate.
—W. E. P. FRENCH

COLORADO

The cattle upon a thousand hills,
And the gold of El Dorado,
All kinds of climate, but darned few ills:
Full glasses—To Colorado!
—W. E. P. FRENCH

IOWA

Iowa—may the affections of her people, like the rivers of her border,
flow to an inseparable union.
—HONORABLE ENOCH W. EASTMAN, former lieutenant governor of
Iowa

KENTUCKY

Kentucky, oh, Kentucky,
How I love your classic shades,
Where flit the fairy figures
Of the star-eyed Southern maids;
Where the butterflies are joying
'Mid the blossoms newly born;
Where the corn is full of kernels,
And the Colonels full of corn!
—WILL LAMPTON

NEW HAMPSHIRE

Live free or die: Death is not the worst of evils.

—GENERAL JOHN STARK, July 31, 1809. Poor health forced Stark, New
Hampshire's most famous soldier of the American Revolution, to decline
an invitation to an anniversary reunion of the Battle of Bennington and to
send his toast by letter.

NEW JERSEY

The fish's blood is very white,
while ours is red as flame.
The "skeeter" has no blood at all,
But gets there just the same.

NORTH CAROLINA

State of the old north star,
Of turpentine and tar,
There's nothing finer
Oh God's green earth than you—
That's why we're drinking to
North Carolina.

—W. E. P. FRENCH

RHODE ISLAND

There's Minnesota's gopher,
    And Texas's lonely star,
And California's golden bear,
    All famed both near and far;
But 'tis not to these I pledge,
    Though all are good, I trow—
I toast old Roger Williams's farm—
    It's called Rhode Island now!

VERMONT

I love Vermont because of her hills and valleys, her scenery and
invigorating climate, but most of all because of her indomitable people.

—CALVIN COOLIDGE

TEMPERANCE

A fig then for Burgundy, Claret or Mountain,
A few scanty glasses must limit your wish.
But here's to the toper that goes to the fountain,
The drinker that verily "drinks like a fish."
—Thomas Hood

Bacchus has drowned more men than Neptune.

Balm of my cares, sweet solace of my toils!
    Hail just benignant!
To the unknown beloved
    This is my good wishes.
—Coffee toast

Black as the devil,
Strong as death,
Sweet as love, and
Hot as hell!
—Coffee toast

Cold water: We never want cash to buy it, we are never ashamed to
ask for it, and never blush to drink it.

Drinking water neither makes a man sick, nor in debt, nor his wife a
widow.

He believes in drinking quantities of water
Undiluted by the essence of the grape.
—Harry Graham

Here's to wine—safer outside than in.

I have found water everywhere that I have traveled.
—Thomas Cook, founder of the international tour company

If you drink like a fish,
Drink what a fish drinks.

Lips that touch wine jelly
Will never touch mine, Nellie.

O' Water for me! Bright Water for me,
And wine for the tremulous debauchee.
—*McGuffey's New Eclectic Speaker*, 1858

Our drink shall be water, bring, sparkling with glee
The gift of our God, and the drink of the free.

There is a devil in every berry of the grape.
—Koran

Water—ever bracing, ever satisfying, ever plenty, and never mocking.

SEE ALSO: *Historic*

THANKSGIVING

Ah! On Thanksgiving day . . .
When the care-wearied man seeks his mother once more,
And the worn matron smiles where the girl smiled before.
What moistens the lips and what brightens the eye?
What calls back the past, like the rich pumpkin pie?
—JOHN GREENLEAF WHITTIER

As we express our gratitude, we must never forget that the highest
appreciation is not to utter words,
but to live by them.
—JOHN FITZGERALD KENNEDY

Bless, O Lord
These delectable vittles,
May they add to the glory
And not to our middles.
—YVONNE WRIGHT, quoted as a
  "Thanksgiving Prayer" in the
  1986 *Reader's Digest* calendar

For turkey braised, the Lord be
praised.

God gave you a gift of 86,400 seconds
today. Have you used one to say "thank you"?
—WILLIAM A. WARD

Here's to the blessings of the year,
Here's to the friends we hold so dear,
To peace on earth, both far and near.

Here's to the day when the Yankees first acknowledged Heaven's good
gifts with Thank'ees.

Here's to the good old turkey
The bird that comes each fall
And with his sweet persuasive meat
Makes gobblers of us all.

May our pleasures be boundless while we have time to enjoy them.

O Thou who has given us so much, mercifully grant us one thing
more—a grateful heart.
—GEORGE HERBERT

Remember God's bounty in the year. String the pearls of His favor.
Hide the dark parts, except so far as they are breaking out in light!
Give this one day to thanks, to joy, to gratitude!
—HENRY WARD BEECHER

Thanksgiving Day is a jewel, to set in the hearts of honest men; but be careful that you do not take the day, and leave out the gratitude.
—E. P. POWELL

Thanksgiving dinners take eighteen hours to prepare. They are consumed in twelve minutes. Half-times take twelve minutes. This is not coincidence.
—ERMA BOMBECK

There is one day that is ours. There is one day when all we Americans who are not self-made go back to the old home to eat saleratus biscuits and marvel how much nearer to the porch the old pump looks than it used to. Thanksgiving Day is the one day that is purely American.
—O. HENRY

To our national birds—
    The American eagle,
    The Thanksgiving turkey:
May one give us peace in all our States—
And the other a piece for all our plates.

When turkey's on the table laid,
    And good things I may scan,
I'm thankful that I wasn't made
A vegetarian.
—EDGAR A. GUEST

TOASTMASTER

Here are four toasts for the person who hardly ever gets toasted.

A toastmaster is a person who eats a meal he doesn't want so he can get up and tell a lot of stories he doesn't remember to people who've already heard them.
—GEORGE JESSEL

An ambidextrous man is he;
    Watch closely, and you'll understand,
A wonder in his way—you see,
    He can toastmast with either hand.

Every rose has its thorn,
    There's fuzz on all the peaches;
There never was a dinner yet
    Without some lengthy speeches.

We'll bless our toastmaster,
Wherever he may roam,
If he'll only cut the speeches short
And let us all go home.

TONGUE TWISTERS

These five traditional toasts not only express a sentiment but also double as sobriety tests.

Here's a health to all those that we love,
Here's a health to all those that love us,
Here's a health to all those that love them that love those
    that love them
that love those that love us.

Here's a health to you and yours who have done such things for us and ours; and when we and ours have it in our powers to do for you and yours what you and yours have done for us and ours, then we and ours will do for you and yours what you and yours have done for us and ours.

Here's to you two and to we two.
If you two love we two
As we two love you two,
Then here's to we four!
But if you two don't love we two
As we two love you two,
Then here's to we two and no more.

Here's to you,
     Here's two to you,
And two to you two, too,
     And to you two, too, here's two.

Tho' a kiss be a-miss,
She who misses the kisses
As Miss without kiss
May miss being a Mrs.
And he who, a-miss,
Thinks both missed and kisses
Will miss Miss and kiss
And the kisses of Mrs.

ULTIMATE TOASTS

The "ultimate" toast is that in which the toast is made, the drink drained in one gulp, and the glass thrown to the floor, against a wall, or into the fire. They were in style when the czars ruled Russia, during the days of George III in England when one toasted the king (as no lesser mortal was supposed to be honored from the same glass), and in the great banquet halls of seventeenth- and eighteenth-century Scotland. Such toasts were commonly proposed with all the participants placing their right foot on their chairs and their left foot on the table.

The traditional Scottish ultimate toast is made with these words:

Up with it, up with it, up with it!
Down it, down it, down it!
From me, from me, from me!
To me, to me, to me!
May all your days be good, my friend!
Take it down!
And no other shall drink from this glass again evermore!

At this point the glass was thrown with gusto over the left shoulder.

Ultimate toasts are now definitely out of style. A pity, because they could do a lot to liven up suburban dinner parties.

WEDDINGS

Weddings require toasts, and best men and other participants are always on the prowl for good raw material to mix into a personalized toast. "Health and happiness" and "May all your troubles be little ones" are the most common wedding toasts, but they have become cliché.

Some other options:

A Second Marriage: To the triumph of hope over experience.
—SAMUEL JOHNSON, 1770

A toast to love and laughter and happily ever after.

A toast to the groom—and discretion to his bachelor friends.

Down the hatch, to a striking match!

Drink, my buddies, drink with discerning,
Wedlock's a lane where there is no turning;
Never was owl more blind than lover;
Drink and be merry, lads; and think it over.
—Bachelor party toast

Grow old with me!
The best is yet to be,
The last of life,
For which, the first is made.
—Robert Browning

Here's to my mother-in-law's daughter,
　　Here's to her father-in-law's son;
And here's to the vows we've just taken,
　　And the life we've just begun.

Here's to the bride and mother-in-law,
Here's to the groom and father-in law,
Here's to sister and brother-in-law,
Here's to friends and friends-in-law,
May none of them need an attorney-at-law.

Here's to the bride and the groom!
　　May you have a happy honeymoon,
May you lead a happy life,
　　May you have a bunch of money soon,
And live without all strife.

Here's to the bride that is to be,
　　Here's to the groom she'll wed,
May all their troubles be light as bubbles
　　Or the feathers that make up their bed!

Here's to the groom with bride so fair,
And here's to the bride with groom so rare!

Here's to the happy man: All the world loves a lover.
—Ralph Waldo Emerson

Here's to the husband—and here's to the wife;
May they remain lovers for life.

Here's to thee and thy folks from me and my folks;
And if thee and they folks love me and my folks
As much as me and my folks love thee and thy folks,
Then there never was folks since folks was folks
Loved me and my folks as much as thee and thy folks.

I drink to myself and one other,
And may that one other be he
Who drinks to himself and one other,
and may that one other be me.

It is written:
"When children find true love,
parents find true joy."
Here's to your joy and ours,
from this day forward
—Parents' toast

Let us toast the health of the bride;
 Let us toast the health of the groom,
Let us toast the person that tied;
 Let us toast every guest in the room.

Look down you gods,
And on this couple drop a blessed crown.
—WILLIAM SHAKESPEARE, *The Tempest*, Act V

Love, be true to her; Life, be dear to her;
Health, stay close to her; Joy, draw near to her;
Fortune, find what you can do for her,
Search your treasure-house through and through for her,
Follow her footsteps the wide world over—
And keep her husband always her lover.
—ANNA LEWIS, "To the Bride"

Marriage: A community consisting of a master, a mistress, and two slaves—making in all, two.
—AMBROSE BIERCE

Marriage has teeth, and him bit very hot.
—Jamaican

Marriage is a wonderful institution, but who wants to live in an institution?
—GROUCHO MARX

May their joys be as bright as the morning, and their sorrows but shadows that fade in the sunlight of love.

May their joys be as deep as the ocean
And their misfortunes as light as the foam.

May we all live to be present at their golden wedding.

May you both live as long as you want to, and want to as long as you live.
—LETITIA BALDRIDGE

May you grow old on one pillow.
—Armenian

May you have enough happiness to keep you sweet; enough trials to keep you strong; enough sorrow to keep you human; enough hope to keep you happy; enough failure to keep you humble; enough success to keep you eager; enough friends to give you comfort; enough faith and courage in yourself, your business, and your country to banish depression; enough wealth to meet your needs; enough determination to make each day a better day than yesterday.

May you have many children
and may they grow as mature in taste
and healthy in color
and as sought after
as the contents of this glass.
—Irish

May you live forever, may I never die.

May your love be as endless as your wedding rings.

May your wedding days be few and your anniversaries many.

Never above you. Never below you. Always beside you.
—WALTER WINCHELL

Of all life's ceremonies that of marriage is the most touching and beautiful. This is the long anticipated climax of girlhood—and boyhood, too—the doorway to true maturity, the farewell to parents as protectors, the acceptance of responsibility.
—AMY VANDERBILT, *Amy Vanderbilt's Etiquette*, 1971

The greatest of all arts is the art of living together.
—WILLIAM LYON PHELPS

There is nothing nobler or more admirable than when two people who see eye to eye keep house as man and wife, confounding their enemies and delighting their friends.
—HOMER, *Odyssey*

These two, now standing hand in hand,
    Remind us of our native land,
For when today they linked their fates,
    They entered the United States.

To my wife—my bride and joy.

To the newlyweds: May "for better or worse" be far better than worse.

Wedlock's like wine—not properly judged of till the second glass.
—ERNEST JARROLD

With this toast the wish is given
From my graying wife and me,
That you'll be as happily married
As we thought that we would be.
—WILLIAM COLE, 1989, who contributed this original toast for this book.
   He called it "a mean one."

Women often weep at weddings, whereas my own instinct is to laugh uproariously and encourage the bride and groom with merry whoops. The sight of people getting married exhilarates me; I think that they are doing a fine thing, and I admire them for it.
—ROBERTSON DAVIES, "Of Nuptial Merriment," in *The Table Talk of Samuel Marchbanks,* 1949

You don't marry one person; you marry three—the person you think they are, the person they are, and the person they are going to become as the result of being married to you.
—RICHARD NEEDHAM, *You and All the Rest,* quoted in *Reader's Digest,* December 1983

You only get married for the second time once.
—GARRISON KEILLOR, quoted in *Forbes,* November 2, 1987

SEE ALSO: *Anniversaries: Husbands; Wives*

WINE

A bottle of good wine, like a good act, shines ever in the retrospect.
—Robert Louis Stevenson, "The Silverado Squatters"

A warm toast.
Good company.
A fine wine.
May you enjoy all three.

Any port in a storm.

Balm of my cares, sweet solace of my toils, Hail justice benignant!
—Thomas Wharton

Clean glasses and old corks.

Comrades, pour the wine tonight
For the parting is with dawn;
Oh, the clink of cups together,
With the daylight coming on!
—Richard Hovey

Count not the cups; not therein lies excess in wine, but in the nature
of the drinker.

Drink wine, and live here blitheful while ye may;
The morrow's life too late is—live today!

For of all labors, none transcend
The works that on the brain depend;
Nor could we finish great designs
Without the power of generous wines.

Give of your wine to others,
   Take of their wine to you.
Toast to life, and be toasted awhile,
   That, and the cask is through.
—JAMES MONROE MCLEAN, *The Book of Wine*

God, in His goodness, sent the grapes
To cheer both great and small;
Little fools will drink too much,
And great fools none at all.

God made Man,
Frail as a Bubble
God made Love
Love made Trouble
God made the Vine
Was it a sin
That Man made Wine
To drown Trouble in?
—OLIVER HERFORD, *The Deb's Dictionary*

Good wine makes good blood;
Good blood causeth good humors;
Good humors cause good thoughts;
Good thoughts bring forth good works;
Good works carry a man to heaven.
Ergo:
Good wine carrieth a man to heaven.
—JAMES HOWELL, to Lord Clifford, early seventeenth century

He that drinks is immortal
For wine still supplies
What age wears away;
How can he be dust
That moistens his clay?
—HENRY PURCELL

He who clinks his cup with mine,
Adds a glory to the wine.
—George Sterling

Here's a bumper of wine; fill thine, fill mine:
Here's a health to old Noah, who planted the vine!
—R. H. Barham

Here's to mine and here's to thine!
    Now's the time to clink it!
Here's a flagon of old wine,
    And here we are to drink it.
—Richard Hovey

Here's to old Adam's crystal ale,
Clear, sparkling and divine,
Fair H_2O, long may you flow,
We drink your health (in wine).
—Oliver Herford

Here's to the man who knows enough
To know he's better without the stuff;
Himself without, the wine within,
So come, me hearties, let's begin.

Here's to the man
Who owns the land
That bears the grapes
That makes the wine
That tastes as good
As this does.

Here's to water, water divine—
    It dews the grapes that give us wine.

I often wonder what the vintners buy
One half so precious as the stuff they sell.
—OMAR KHAYYÁM

Let those who drink not, but austerely dine, dry up in law; the Muses
smell of wine.
—HORACE

Then a smile, and a glass, and a toast and a cheer,
For all the good wine, and we've some of it here.
—OLIVER WENDELL HOLMES

This bottle's the sun of our table,
      His beams are rosy wine;
We, plants that are not able
      Without his help to shine.

This wine is full of gases
      Which are to me offensive,
It pleases all you asses
      Because it is expensive.
—A. P. HERBERT

This wine is too good for toast-drinking, my dear. You don't want to
mix emotions up with a wine like that. You lose the taste.
—ERNEST HEMINGWAY, Count Mippipopolous to Brett,
   in *The Sun Also Rises*

To the big-bellied bottle.

When I die—the day be far!
Should the potters make ajar
Out of this poor clay of mine,
Let the jar be filled with wine!

When wine enlivens the heart
May friendship surround the table.

Wine and women—May we always have a taste for both.

Who was it, I pray,
On the wedding day
Of the Galilean's daughter
With a touch divine
Turned in wine
Six buckets of *filtered* water?
—OLIVER WENDELL HOLMES

Wine improves with age—I like it more the older I get.

SEE ALSO: *Alliterative; Biblical; Celia's Toast (with Variations);
Champagne; General; Libations; Prohibition; Revelry*

WIVES

A good wife and health
Are a man's best wealth.

A health to our widows. If they ever
marry again, may they do as well!

Here's to the man who takes a wife,
Let him make no mistake:
For it makes a lot of difference
Whose wife it is you take.

Late last night I slew my wife,
Stretched her on the parquet flooring:
I was loath to take her life,
But I had to stop her snoring.

To our wives and sweethearts. May they never meet!

SEE ALSO: *Anniversaries; Weddings; Woman and Women*

WOMAN AND WOMEN

Drink to fair woman, who, I think,
  Is most entitled to it;
For if anything drives men to drink,
  She certainly can do it.

Fill, fill, fill a brimming glass
Each man toast his favorite lass,
He who flinches is an ass,
Unworthy of love or wine.

Here's looking at you, dear!
Though I should pour a sea of wine,
My eyes would thirst for more.

Here's to God's first thought, "Man"!
Here's to God's second thought, "Woman"!
Second thoughts are always best,
So here's to Woman!

Here's to the gladness of her gladness when she's glad,
Here's to the sadness of her sadness when she's sad;
But the gladness of her gladness,
And the sadness of her sadness,
Are not in it with the madness of her madness when she's mad.

Here's to the lasses we've loved, my lad,
Here's to the lips we've pressed;
    For of kisses and lasses,
Like liquor in glasses,
    The last is always the best.

I have never studied the art of paying compliments to women, but I must say that if all that has been said by orators and poets since the creation of the world in praise of women were applied to the women of America, it would not do them justice. God bless the women of America.
—ABRAHAM LINCOLN

Let her be clumsy, or let her be slim,
    Young or ancient, I care not a feather;
So fill up a bumper, nay, fill to the brim,
    Let us toast all the ladies together.

Of all your beauties, one by one,
    I pledge, dear, I am thinking;
Before the tale were well begun
    I had been dead of drinking.

They talk about a woman's sphere as though it had a limit;
There's not a place on earth or heaven,
There's not a task to mankind given,
There's not a blessing or a woe,
There's not a whispered yes or no,
There's not a life or birth,
That has a feather's weight of worth—
    Without a woman in it.

To the ladies, God bless them,
May nothing distress them.

To the woman in her higher, nobler aspects, whether wife, widow, grass widow, mother-in-law, hired girl, telegraph operator, telephone helloer, queen, book agent, wet nurse, stepmother, boss, professional fat woman, professional double-headed woman, or professional beauty—God bless her.
—Mark Twain

'Tween woman and wine a man's lot is to smart,
For wine makes his head ache, and woman his heart.

We've toasted the mother and daughter
We've toasted the sweetheart and wife;
But somehow we missed her,
Our dear little sister—
The joy of another man's life.

What, sir, would people of the earth be without woman? They would be scarce, sir, almighty scarce.
—Mark Twain

SEE ALSO: *General; Love; Lust; Parents; Weddings; Wives*

WORLD'S WORST TOASTS

Over time, the human mind has composed a mind-numbing collection of bad toasts. Even the most seemingly narrow category of toast is liable to have a set of genuine groaners. For instance, it's difficult to decide which of these three toasts to those in the hardware business is the worst:

To the hardware dealer—who, if he keeps hammering away on the level, will nail plenty of customers, providing he's on the square. That's plane to see.

Or,

Here's to the fellow who can stand on his own two feet and face the world squarely without blinking an eye. He calls a spade a spade.

Or,

To those in the hardware trade—although they profess to honesty, they sell iron and steel for a living.

Here is a mercifully small selection of the author's all-star best of the worst.

A hobo is seen by the side of the road running a lighted match up and down the seams of his shirt by a passerby, who asks, "What are you doing?" The hobo replies, "Toasting the visitors."

A pretzel and un stein o'peer,
And thou, mit sixteen kinder,
Ach, my lieber frau,
Sitting beside me, those garden in—
Ach! Dat were baradise already now!

A wee little dog passed a wee little tree.
Said the wee little tree, "Won't you have one on me?"
"No," said the little dog, no bigger than a mouse.
"I just had one on the house."

An amoeba named Joe and his brother
Went out drinking toasts to each other.
    In the midst of their quaffing
    They split their sides laughing
And found that each one was a mother.

Dismay to unskilled surgeons—who, like the nocturnal feline, mew-till-late and destroy patients.

Here's to love, ain't life grand!
Just got a divorce from my old man.
I laughed and laughed at the judge's decision;
He gave him all the kids,
And none of 'em were his'n!

Here's to the Laplanders—cold and haughty! And here's to their
southern sisters—not quite so much so.

I feel just like a loaf of bread. Wherever I go, they toast me.

I propose a little toast.
You'll have to do better than that—I'm hungry.

Let us drink a toast to the queer old dean.
—Toast allegedly proposed by the Reverend William A. Spooner to Queen
   Victoria, his "dear old queen." Spooner, of course, was responsible for
   innumerable "tips of the slongue."

May the village "belle" never be too long in the clapper!
—Old English

May those who'd be rude to American roses
Feel a thorn's fatal prick in their lips and their noses.

O Woman! Lovely Woman!
You're just like a gun;
You're loaded up with powder
And wadded most a ton
You set your cap with care,
And with a "bang" you slyly shoot
Your eyeballs at his stare. Oh Fudge!

To hay fever—here's looking at-choooo!

To the one we love—when she is our toast, we don't want any but her.

232

When the governor of the Virgin Islands was visiting Washington, D.C., the toastmaster became flustered during his introduction and announced, "It's a great pleasure to present the virgin of Governor's Island."

—*Teacher's Treasury of Stories for Every Occasion,* quoted in *Reader's Digest,* April 1985

Woman's hair; beautiful hair,
　　What words of praise I'd utter—
But, oh, how sick it makes me feel,
　　To find it in the butter.

Acknowledgments

I break my bones before you.
—*Japanese toast referring to
the severest form of genuflection*

The idea for my toast collection first came to me during the summer of 1977, after I had bought, for a nickel, a slim volume of toasts at a library book sale in Maine. That book, which was published in 1906, got me started as a compiler of toasts, and so my first indebtedness must go to Idelle Phelps, author of *Your Health!*

Beyond Ms. Phelps a number of contemporary individuals and institutions have joined my campaign to revive the toast. First, I am obliged to a legion of reference librarians, spread geographically from Boston to San Diego, who helped me get a bead on my dusty quarry. The staffs of the Library of Congress, the Wayne State University Folklore Archives, the Tamony Collection of the University of Missouri, and the Public Library of Cincinnati and Hamilton County were extraordinarily helpful in this regard. Al Durante, a gentleman with A. Smith Bowman, the company that produces Virginia Gentleman whiskey, allowed me access to his fine collection of toasts for my original collection, as did Jack McGowan from Dublin. Thanks also to Paul H. Emerson.

I would also like to thank a number of friends, including Frank C. Dorsey, Thomas B. Allen, the late John Masterman, Randy Roberts, Bob Skole, Joseph C. Goulden, Florenz Baron, the late Bob Snider, Elaine Viets, the late James Thorpe III, Bill Cole, Bill Tammeaus, and Mariquita Mullan, for their contributions, not the least of which was their enthusiasm. Special thanks to Nelson Eddy for his help in rounding up celebrity toasts. Neda Abrams of Guinness and M. K. Paskus, protocol officer at the U.S. Department of State, must also be singled out for their help. My late mother, Isabelle C. Dickson, did her usual fine job as research assistant—in this case coming up with a dozen or so of this book's best toasts. Finally, thanks to Nancy, to whom all the nice toasts under "Love" apply (to say nothing of a few under "Lust").

Here's to all!

Selected Bibliography

The cause of Bibliomania all over the world.
—*Toast of the Roxburghe Club, 1812*

More than three hundred sources were consulted for this collection, including many old books and booklets with the word *toast* in the title. Here is a selected list of the most useful sources.

Abel, Ernest L. *Alcohol: Wordlore and Folklore*. Buffalo, NY: Prometheus Books, 1987.

Alderson, William A. *Here's to You*. New York: Dodge Publishing Co., 1907.

Allen, Steve. *Curses; or, How Never to Be Foiled Again*. Los Angeles: J. P. Tarcher, 1973.

Anderson, Will. *The Beer Book*. Princeton, NJ: Pyne Press, 1973.

Antrim, Minna Thomas. *A Book of Toasts*. Philadelphia: Henry Altemus Co., 1902.

Auden, W. H. *The Oxford Book of Light Verse*. Oxford University Press, 1938.

Aye, John. *Humor of Drinking*. London: Universal Publishing Co., 1934.

Benham, Sir Gurney. *Benham's Book of Quotations, Proverbs and Household Words*. New York: G. P. Putnam's, 1936.

Bennett, James O'Donnell. *When Good Fellows Get Together*. Chicago: Reilly and Britton Co., 1908.

Berman, Frederick. *The Complete Toastmaster*. London: Blandford Press, 1953.

Birmingham, Frederick. *Falstaff's Complete Beer Book*. New York: Award Books, 1970.

Braude, Jacob. *Complete Speaker's and Toastmaster's Library*. 8 vols. Englewood Cliffs, NJ: Prentice-Hall Inc., 1957.

Brewer, E. Cobham. *Dictionary of Phrase and Fable*. Philadelphia: Henry Altamus, 1898.

Bridges, John, and Bryan Curtis. *Gentleman Raises His Glass*. Nashville, TN: Rutledge Hill Press, 2005.

Brooks, Fred Emerson. *Cream Toasts*. Chicago: Forbes and Co., 1915.

Butler, Anthony. *The Book of Blarney*. New York: Dell Publishing Co., 1969.

Case, Carleton B. *The Big Toast Book*. Chicago: Shrewsbury Publishing, 1927.

Chase, Edith Lea, and Captain W. E. P. French. *Waes Hael: The Book of Toasts; Being, for the Most Part, Bubbles Gathered from the Wine of Others' Wit, with, Here and There, an Occasional Humbler Globule Believed to Be More or Less Original*. New York: Grafton Press, 1905.

Chethik, Neil. "The Best Man Should Keep Toast Simple." *Plain Dealer*, June 2, 1996.

Clode, Edward J. *2088 Jokes, Toasts and Anecdotes*. New York: Grosset and Dunlap, 1921.

Cobb, Irvin S. *Irvin S. Cobb's Own Recipe Book*. Frankfort, KY: Frankfort Distilleries, 1934.

Connelly, Bertha, and Helen Ramsey. *Modern Toasts for All Occasions*. Minneapolis, MN: Northwestern Press, n.d.

Copeland, Lewis, and Faye Copeland. *10,000 Jokes, Toasts and Stories*. Garden City, NY: Halcyon House, 1940.

Davis, Bert. *Crisp Toasts*. New York: H. M. Caldwell Co., 1907.

Dodge, W. W. *The Fraternal and Modern Banquet Orator*. Burlington, IA: W. W. Dodge, 1903.

Dwiggins, Clare Victor. *Toast Book*. Philadelphia: John C. Winston Co., 1905.

Edmund, Peggy, and H. W. Williams. *Toaster's Handbook*. New York: H. W. Wilson and Co., 1914.

Einhorn, Benjamin. *Jewish Curses for All Occasions*. New York: Ace, 1970.

Eleven Cellars Wines. *A Book of Wine and Toasts*. Delano, CA: Eleven Cellars Wines, n.d.

Epsy, Willard R. *The Life and Works of Mr. Anonymous*. New York: Hawthorne Books, 1977.

Erdoes, Richard. *Saloons of the Old West*. New York: Knopf, 1979.

Evans, William R., and Andrew Frothingham. *Crisp Toasts: Wonderful Words That Add Wit and Class to Every Time You Raise Your Glass*. New York: St. Martin's Press, 2007.

Fenno, R. F. *Toasts and Maxims*. New York: R. F. Fenno and Co., 1908.

Filson, Jon. "When 'Cheers' Is Not Enough." *Toronto Star*, September 15, 2004.

Fleming, Atheron. *Gourmet's Book of Food and Drink*. London: Bodley Head, 1933.

Fougner, G. Selmer. *Along the Wine Trail*. New York: New York Sun Publishing Co., 1935.

Frank, Catherine. *Quotations for All Occasions*. New York: Columbia University Press, 2000.

French, Richard Valpy. *Nineteen Centuries of Drink in England*. London: Longmans, Green, and Co., 1884.

————. *The History of Toasting; or, Drinking of Healths in England*. London: National Temperance Publication Depot, n.d.

Friedman, Edward L. *Toastmaster's Treasury*. New York: Harper and Row, 1960.

Friedman, Gil. *A Dictionary of Love*. Arcata, CA: Yara Press, 1990.

Fuller, Edmund. *Thesaurus of Epigrams*. New York: Crown, 1943.

Fulmer, Dave. *A Gentleman's Guide to Toasting*. Lynchburg, TN: Oxmoor House for Jack Daniel's Distillery, 1990.

Garrison, Robert L. *Here's to You! 354 Toasts You Can Use Today for Parties, Holidays, and Public Affairs*. New York: Crown, 1980.

Gayre, G. R. *Wassail! In Mazers of Mead*. London: Phillimore and Co., 1964.

Glover, Ellye Howell. *Dame Curtsey's Book of Novel Entertainments for Every Day of the Year*. Chicago: A. C. McClurg and Co., 1927.

Gray, Arthur. *Toasts and Tributes: A Happy Book of Good Cheer, Good Health, Good Speed, Devoted to the Blessings and Comforts of Life South of the Stars*. Detroit and New York: Rhode and Haskins, 1904.

Guensburg, Carol. "Cheers to the Maker of Memorable Toasts." *Milwaukee Journal*, August 4, 1994.

Hackwood, Frederick W. *Inns, Ales, and Drinking Customs of Old England*. London: T. Fisher Unwin, 1909.

Hartman, J. F. *Spice and Parody*. New York: Outing Publishing Co., 1906.

Harvey, James Clarence. *Over the Nuts and Wine*. Boston: H. M. Caldwell, 1906.

Harwell, Richard Barksdale. *The Mint Julep*. Savannah, GA: Beehive Press, 1975.

Haverson, James P. *Sour Sonnets of a Sorehead*. Boston: H. M. Caldwell Co., 1908.

Henry, Lewis C. *Toasts for All Occasions*. Garden City, NY: Halcyon House, 1949.

Herford, Oliver, and John Cecil Clay. *Happy Days*. New York: Mitchell Kennerley, 1917.

Herman, Jeff, and Deborah Herman. *Toasts for All Occasions*. Franklin Lakes, NJ: Career Press, 1998.

Hewitt, W. C. *The Best After-Dinner Stories and How to Tell Them*. Chicago: Charles T. Powner Co., 1946.

Hughes, T. *The Toastmaster's Guide*. London: Hughes, 1806.

The Humming Bird; or, New American Songster; With Modern Toasts and Sentiments. Boston: Spotswood and Etheridge, 1798.

Huston, Mervyn J. *Toasts to the Bride and How to Propose Them*. Rutland, VT: Charles Tuttle, 1968.

Iverson, William. *O the Times! O the Manners!* New York: William Morrow and Co., 1965.

Jeffery, Barbara. *Wedding Speeches and Toasts*. Slough, Berkshire, England: W. Foulsam and Co., 1971.

Kaser, Arthur Leroy. *Good Toasts and Funny Stories*. Chicago: T. S. Denison and Co., 1923.

Kearney, Paul W. *Toasts and Anecdotes*. New York: Edward J. Clode, 1923.

Koken, John M. *Here's to It!* New York: A. S. Barnes, 1960.

Lewis, E. C. *Toasts for All Occasions*. Boston: Mutual Book Co., 1903.

Lewis, E. L. *Everybody Up—A Book of Toasts*. Boston: H. M. Caldwell, 1909.

Loots, Barbara Kunz. *The Little Book of Toasts*. Kansas City: Hallmark, 1975.

Lowe, Paul E. *The 20th-Century Book of Toasts*. Philadelphia: David McKay, 1910.

Madison, Janet. *Toasts You Ought to Know*. Chicago: Reilly and Britton Co., 1908.

Marchant, W. T. *In Praise of Ale*. London: George Redway, 1888.

Masello, Robert. "Things Your Dad Never Taught You." *Men's Health*, April 1996.

Matheney, Dave. "Toasts of the Times: May Your Credit Rating Always Be High and Your Cholesterol Level Low." *Minneapolis Star Tribune*, December 31, 1991.

McClure, John, and William Rose Benet. *The Stag's Hornbook*. New York: Knopf, 1945.

McCord, David. *What Cheer.* New York: Coward-McCann, 1945.

McIvor, Ivor Ben. *Scottish Toasts.* New York: H. M. Caldwell, 1908.

McLean, James Monroe. *The Book of Wine.* Philadelphia: Dorrance and Co., 1934.

Morgan, Philip. "A Good Toast Never Goes Stale." *Tampa Tribune*, April 14, 1966.

Morewood, Samuel. *Inventions and Customs of Ancient and Modern Nations in the Manufacture and Use of Inebriating Liquors.* Dublin, 1838.

Morrison, Lillian. *Yours Till Niagara Falls.* New York: Thomas Y. Crowell Co., 1950.

Muller, Helen M. *Still More Toasts.* New York: H. W. Wilson Co., 1932.

Murphy, J. F. *Five Hundred Popular and Up-to-Date Toasts.* Boston: J. F. Murphy, n.d.

Nesbit, Wilbur. *The Loving Cup: Original Toasts by Original Folks.* Chicago: P. F. Volland and Co., 1909.

Nickell, Colonel Joe. *The Kentucky Mint Julep.* Lexington: University Press of Kentucky, 2003.

Ott, Irv. *Popular Toasts.* Baltimore: Phoenix Publishing Co., 1904.

Perret, Gene, with Terry Perret Martin. *Roasts and Toasts.* New York: Sterling, 1997.

Phelps, Idelle. *Your Health!* Philadelphia: George W. Jacobs, 1906.

Prochnow, Herbert V. *Toastmaster's Handbook.* New York: Prentice-Hall, 1949.

Proskauer, Julien J. *What'll You Have?* New York: A. L. Burt, 1933.

Prynne, William. *Healthes Sicknesse.* London, 1628.

Pudney, John. *The Harp Book of Toasts.* London: Harp Lager, 1963.

Ramsay, William. *A Book of Toasts.* New York: Dodge Publishing Co., 1906.

Reynolds, Cuyler. *The Banquet Book.* New York: G. P. Putnam, 1902.

Rice, Wallace, and Frances Rice. *Toasts and Tipple: A Book of Conviviality.* New York: M. A. Donohue and Co., 1914.

"The Right Way to Propose a Toast." *Fresno Bee*, December 30, 1998.

Roach, J. *The Royal Toastmaster.* London, 1791.

Robinson, Gaile. "Raise a Glass; Don't Burn the Toast." *Bergen County (NJ) Record*, May 2, 1999.

Rodgers, H. A. *Toasts and Cocktails.* St. Louis, MO: Shallcross Printing and Stationary Co., 1905.

Rosten, Leo. *The Giant Book of Laughter*. New York: Bonanza, 1989.

Rowe, Colonel William H. Jr. *Campaign Verse and Toasts*. Albany, NY: J. B. Lyon and Co., 1908.

Schmidt, William. *The Flowing Bowl*. New York: Charles L. Webster, 1892.

Scrivener, Matthew. *A Treatise Against Drunkennesse: Described in Its Nature, Kindes Effects and Causes, Especially That of Drinking of Healths*. London: Printed for Charles Brown, Cambridge bookseller, 1685.

Shane Na Gael [pseud.]. *Irish Toasts*. New York: H. M. Caldwell, 1908.

Simon, Andrew Lewis. *Drink*. New York: Horizon Press, 1953.

Stafford, William Young. *Toasts and Speeches*. Chicago: Frederick J. Drake and Co., 1902.

Sullivan, James. *Smart Toasts for the Smart Set*. New York: M. J. Ivers, 1903.

Sutherland, Natalie M. *Toasts, Jokes and Limericks*. New York: Reader Mail, 1937.

Toasts. St. Louis, MO: William J. Lemp Brewing Co., 1896, 1908.

The Toasts of the Rump-Steak Club. London: Printed and sold by the booksellers of London and Westminster, 1734.

Viets, Elaine. "Here's Mud in Your Eye." *St. Louis Post Dispatch*, December 26, 1976.

Waters, Margaret. *Toasts*. New York: Barse and Hopkins, 1909.

Watney, John. *Mother's Ruin: A History of Gin*. London: Peter Owen, 1976.

Williams, Victor W. *"Hello Bill" Toasts*. San Francisco: Whitaker and Ray Co., 1903.

Woolard, Sam F. *Good Fellowship*. Wichita, KS: Goldsmith Woolard Publishing Co., 1904.

Wright, Richardson. *The Bed-Book of Eating and Drinking*. Philadelphia: J. B. Lippincott, 1943.

Zabriskie, George A. *The Bon Vivant's Companion*. Ormand Beach, FL: privately printed, 1948.

Zucco, Tom. "A Toast to Toasts." *St. Petersburg Times*, December 28, 1994.

INTERNET RESOURCES

Two relevant Web sites are maintained by the author. The site http://toastsbook.com supports this book and serves as an interactive location for collecting toasts for future editions.

The author's general Web site is http://pauldicksonbooks.com, which lists, among other things, author appearances. Readers can also contact the author by mail at P.O. Box 280, Garrett Park, MD 20896.

Toastmasters International, http://toastmasters.org, is a natural destination for those wishing to learn more about toasting and to meet with others who are interested in public speaking.

With the Internet came a proliferation of fill-in-the-blank toasts that can be had without charge and are composed of light introductions and serious endings. These became so common so quickly that one can get a laugh just by reading the toast with the fill-in-the-blank lines unchanged:

> Excuse me. Would anybody mind if I took this time to wish Ms. Bride and Mr. Groom a happy half-hour anniversary? (Laughter, applause) I would like to say thank you to Mr. and Mrs. Bride's Parents for all that you've done to make this the special day that it is. And, of course, my gratitude to Mr. and Mrs. Groom's Parents for all of your support and all that you've done to make this, by all accounts, the perfect day. And finally, thank you, Mr. Groom for making such a good choice for the best man.

A number of Web sites offer canned wedding toasts as well as services that offer to write a toast for a fee.

Some hilarious toasts can be watched on You Tube (http://youtube.com)—although many of them are better viewed as theater than as useful toasts.

A NOTE ON THE AUTHOR

PAUL DICKSON is the author of more than fifty books. He concentrates on writing about the American language, baseball, and twentieth-century history. He is a collector of words and wordplay whose other works of this nature include *Words*, *Names*, *Jokes*, *Slang*, and *Family Words*, among others. He is a contributing editor for Dover Publications and *Washingtonian* magazine. His most recent books are *The Dickson Baseball Dictionary–Third Edition*, *A Dictionary of the Space Age*, and *The Unwritten Rules of Baseball*.